THE ROYAL MARSDEN HOSPITAL
Manual of Core Care Plans for Cancer Nursing

D1385946

THE ROYAL MARSDEN HOSPITAL

Manual of Core Care Plans for Cancer Nursing

ALISON RICHARDSON
BN MSc RGN ONCCert

Macmillan Lecturer in Cancer Nursing and Palliative Care
Department of Nursing Studies, King's College,
University of London
Formerly Sister, Sarcoma and Melanoma Unit,
The Royal Marsden Hospital, London

with a Foreword by
ROBERT TIFFANY
OBE RGN RCNT FRCN
Director of In-patient Services/Chief Nursing Officer,
The Royal Marsden Hospital, London

Scutari Press · London

Scutari Press, a division of Scutari Projects Ltd,
is the publishing arm of the Royal College of
Nursing, London

First published 1992

British Library Cataloguing-in-publication-Data
Richardson, Alison
    The Royal Marsden Hospital book of core care plans
    for cancer nursing
    I. Title
    616.99
    ISBN 1 871364 68 X

Printed and bound in Great Britain by
Biddles Ltd, Guildford and King's Lynn

CONTENTS

CONTENTS

CONTENTS

ACKNOWLEDGEMENTS

While working on this book I have received tremendous support and encouragement from colleagues at The Royal Marsden Hospital. I am particularly indebted to Robert Tiffany for allowing me the time to complete this work and to Phylip Pritchard and Mark Darley for their inspiration and constructive criticism; Tonia Dawson, Jacqueline Moore and Robert Tunmore offered advice on sexuality, biological therapies and information-giving respectively.

I would like in addition to offer my thanks to David Proudfoot, Ann Ryan and Katy Parris who battled with my indecipherable prose, translating it into legible type, and to Patrick West who provided support and guidance in the ways of publishing.

FOREWORD

The idea for this manual arose out of the increasing need to document nursing care clearly, accurately and concisely. The nursing process is familiar to most nurses as they have, in the main, been working with it for a number of years, but a major complaint appears to be that it takes a great deal of time to document the planning and evaluation of care. In an ever more technological and pressured clinical environment, time is a precious commodity. This manual is designed to address this matter in part. *The Royal Marsden Hospital Manual of Core Care Plans* is designed to offer nurses a text on which they might wish to base care plans for their clinical areas. These plans have been carefully and painstakingly researched and collated to ensure that the highest quality of care can be offered to patients which is accurately recorded. The plans are not intended to replace the planning of care that must take place in response to complex patient problems and needs, but they will provide an invaluable aid to nurses needing to document the care required for more commonly encountered problems in order to maximise efficient use of their time. The researched and clinically tested basis of these care plans will give the resultant nursing care a rational theoretical basis. The synthesis of theory and practice leads in my view to good nursing care.

It gives me pleasure to commend *The Royal Marsden Hospital Manual of Core Care Plans* to you. I would be pleased to hear from practising nurses how well the plans aid their work so that subsequent editions of this manual can be updated.

ROBERT TIFFANY
Director of In-Patient Services/Chief Nursing Officer

Introduction

INTRODUCTION

The motivation and interest for this present work arose with the realisation that cancer patients may experience common needs and problems when undergoing treatment for their disease. Core care plans may be utilised to produce realistic and workable guides to nursing practice.

As early as 1973 Virginia Henderson recommended that nurses make written plans for all patients, advocating a problem solving approach in order to co-ordinate care (Henderson, 1973). It is now generally recognised that the development of individualised care plans are necessary, in part, to facilitate the provision of optimum patient care. This is reinforced by Grant (1975) when she states the 'nursing care plan provides a tool for individualised care'. The use of a nursing care plan, integral to the nursing process, supported by methods of organising care, such as team nursing, primary nursing or patient allocation which promote individual responsibility for decisions, Clarke (1978) insists, will lead to care which is well adapted to individual patient needs. In contrast, management of work utilising a task-centred approach to care creates routines based on ward custom and possible poor planning of care which may lead to care which is ill adapted to patients' individual need. This is illustrated in several descriptive studies which form part of the Royal College of Nursing Study of Nursing Care Series, for example in relation to pre-operative care (Hamilton-Smith, 1972) and bowel care (Wright, 1974). A regard for the whole person and individual differences is now prevalent, and as Meyers (1972) suggests nurses have come to accept and understand the rationale behind the provision of nursing care that is tailored to an individual's wants and needs.

By accepting that no two patients are the same it is logical to assume that their care will reflect this. Despite this, a danger exists wherein nurses can lose sight of some common characteristics, needs and problems. Martin and Glasper (1986) emphasise the uniqueness of human behaviour and experience but suggest there is a tendency to underestimate human commonalities. A rational approach to planning care can be evolved from consideration of the similarities as well as differences – a core care plan.

Core Care Plans

A number of definitions has been offered on the nature of a core care plan. Meyers (1972) describes the use of standard care routines and writes of 'a specific core of nursing activities that is appropriate for the use of patients who are progressing within expected norms for the treatment of the disease process'. The plan outlines the basic care common to all patients with the same condition. This is not viewed as a standard care plan, which may produce dehumanised, uniform or task-centred care, but as an approach that allows for the planning of care that is founded on predictable outcomes, on which individual care can be built.

Core care plans have been identified by Glasper *et al* (1987) as plans of care based on an explicit model of nursing that deal with a particular problem or need, and which are often allied to an agreed policy, or procedure with medical colleagues. The plans identify commonalities in patient care for high priority problems in which there is a high level of agreement about appropriate nursing actions. Four main advantages were outlined as being relevant to the clinical setting. Core care plans:

1 enable the nurse to escape paper work
2 enable the nurse to identify crucial and immediate care
3 promote greater understanding of the rationale for care
4 facilitate the identification of appropriate methods of audit and quality assurance.

The development of a comprehensive, but not exhaustive, series of core care plans was undertaken with a hope of providing a stronger link between nursing theory and clinical practice. Perceived constraints to effective care planning were identified as:

1 the nurses' lack of knowledge, language and ability to 'think nursing'
2 an unwillingness to document repetitive and similar nursing tasks
3 the volume of care encountered in large hospitals with rapid turnover of patients, making formulation of plans immensely difficult.

Wright (1987) and his staff developed core care plans as a response to the need to reduce writing time and a desire to give patients access to their care plans. Wright acknowledges the often complex nature of care plan documentation, and in endeavouring to reduce the time taken to complete a plan in a busy clincial environment, he devised a series of core care plans which he defined as detailed plans which express precisely and unambiguously the care given by nurses.

A few main points were identified in relation to the plans which were developed:

1 the plans were to be used in conjunction with a primary nursing system;
2 the plans were detailed and unambiguous;
3 the language of the plans was simple to allow patients to read and understand them (Wright, 1990).

Many would perhaps agree that the denial of individual difference and patient preference militates against both the patient and the professional nurse. Wright (1990) comments that in his opinion, initial reservations about core care plans becoming standard care plans, such as patients being in danger of having the same routine applied to them regardless of personal need, have not so far materialised.

McFarlane and Casteldine (1982) describe a standard care plan as basically a 'checklist of the routine care which it is proposed to give a patient irrespective of his specific needs' (p 87) and are often used in conjunction with individualised plans of care. This approach is seen to be helpful in cutting down unnecessary written work and in establishing safe and helpful routines of nursing care, and is perhaps most useful for standard procedures such as pre- and post-operative care or for specifying safety in certain procedures. The use by nurses of standard care plans has also been commented upon by Nicholls and Barstow (1980) who advocate that they may be utilised as tools for patient care.

The idea that pre-written plans stifle creativity and promote task-centred care could be advanced as a criticism of core care plans. Any problem-solving system is only as good as the problem-solving ability of the nurse using it. Hurst (1985) provides evidence that the success of the nursing process is dependent upon the users' problem-solving ability, and failures to individualise care leave open to question how the nurse is being educated to provide such care. Fundamental to the provision of intelligent and sensitive care is the process of effective decision-making and this skill must be fostered in all nurses. Wright (1987) argues that a nurse who internalises the necessity to meet individual needs will always deliver care on an individual and planned basis, sensitive to potential demands and responsive to new situations.

Core care plans should never be a substitute for the activity of gathering information to facilitate the synthesis of comprehensive and innovative plans of care. An assessment strategy militates against the individual patient's identity and personal needs being obscured and a thorough evaluation should prevent the propagation of ineffective care.

From the small amount of literature available on core care plans, it appears that a core care plan can provide an expression of precise and unambiguous common care points. These may be referred to by the nurse involved in the provision of nursing interventions for patients undergoing specific treatment plans or exhibiting particular problems or needs. This need not detract from or suppress the cognitive skills or creative ability of the nurse in formulating individual approaches to patient care in collaboration with the patient, and members of other health care professions.

Standards of Care

Nursing care plans are only a means to an end, that of providing individualised nursing care, not solely an end in themselves. Shea (1986) emphasises that a good care plan does not ensure a high quality of care, nor has it been demonstrated that the lack of a care plan will result in a diminished quality of nursing care.

Redfern and Norman (1990) state that nurses have been struggling with the ways and means of measuring quality for many years, and feel that the endeavour has never had the sense of urgency it has today. An increasing amount of literature is indeed available, discussing what will be evaluated and how the evaluation shall be done (for example Wright 1984 and Luker 1984).

The setting of standards may form part of the cycle of events leading to quality assurance. Crow (1981) views a standard as 'the level which others accept as the baseline for good practice . . . a measure to which others conform'. Kitson (1984, 1989) outlines the underlying values and beliefs regarding quality and the setting of standards for nursing care. The document *A Framework for Quality – a Patient Centered Approach to Quality Assurance in Health Care* describes the approach used in designing and setting up the Royal College of Nursing Dynamic Standard Setting System which may be used by practitioners to set, monitor and evaluate their own standards of care. The system is based on shared objective setting and on agreeing achievable standards of care. In the area of cancer care, work on the formulation of standards for cancer nursing is well advanced. Nationally, the Royal College of Nursing Cancer Nursing Society has published its work in the form of a national standard document which outlines standards for good practice in cancer nursing, supported by a philosophy statement which identifies beliefs and values that underpin excellence in cancer nursing.

In 1989 The Royal Marsden Hospital began a clinical standard of care project, under the guidance of a quality assurance officer. The objective of this project was to collate a number of clinical standards of care (for example, constipation, nausea and vomiting, chronic pain) that related specifically to the needs and requirements of patients with cancer, written by practising experts in cancer nursing and rehabilitative care. These standards define the resources required to achieve the determined level of care, the professional practice necessary to achieve it and the expected outcomes (Luthert, 1990).

The model chosen from which to sketch out a usable framework was a synthesis of Donabedian's (1966) and Wilson's (1987) work. The notions of 'structure', 'process' and 'outcome' were taken from Donabedian's papers, but the conversion of these abstract concepts into a more concrete and definable checklist came from Wilson.

'Structure' translated into 'resources' and includes three major areas: 1 people, 2 equipment and 3 environment. 'Process' translated into 'practice' and includes aspects of the 'nursing process' in terms of assessment, planning, implementation of care and evaluation. 'Outcomes' remain 'outcomes' but become the link between the use of resources, the following of professional practice and the standards of care, and define where these data should come from – from the documentation of care, from the patient and from the professional involved in the care of that patient. In future, the outcomes will be incorporated into a detailed measurement tool to assess the quality of care (Luthert, 1991).

It is implicit that these standards will form the basis of nursing and the rehabilitation care audit to assess the quality of care both given to and received by patients at The Royal Marsden Hospital.

A standard, as envisaged by Luthert (1990), addresses in part dimensions of 'professional' practice. The core plans outlined in this handbook may add an additional dimension to this component of the standard, and provide a partial answer to the question many nurses should ask 'What do I need to do in order to achieve a prescribed standard of care?'

The Manual

The core care plans presented in the following pages address commonly occurring cancer treatment strategies and adverse responses resulting from such interventions. In presenting these plans it is recognised that cancer patients undergoing similar treatments have common as well as unique care needs. The core care plan may direct the carer to reflect upon those aspects of care which are common while leaving them free to develop individual care as they deem appropriate in partnership with the patient. The plans are intended as suggestions for care to be considered, but not necessarily completed on every occasion for every patient.

Prior to utilising the suggestions it is considered that an intelligent, perceptive and skilled assessment is paramount to the determination of a need for nursing care. A crucial element in the delivery of effective care is the relevance of care based on a thorough assessment. The necessity for evaluation is also acknowledged. There must be a detailed examination of the outcomes achieved following utilisation of some or all of the suggestions.

The core care plans should be seen as an information resource and educational tool for nurses responsible for delivering care to cancer patients. They should not be seen in isolation, but interpreted using:

1 general and specific knowledge of cancer and cancer nursing
2 previous experience
3 specific personal patient information
4 recognition of an individual professional nurse's creativity and problem-solving ability.

These care plans are intended to be a realistic guide for practising nurses. The plans are essentially practical. They are not definitive statements and as such should provide a flexible basis for local care planning in a wide variety of clinical settings using differing systems for the organisation of care.

These care plans do not conform to a specific model of nursing. This decision is quite deliberate. Models developed by nurse theorists and practising nurses are now becoming more widely used, utilisation of one of these models in particular would have made the care plans difficult to use in areas that favoured another model from that chosen.

The author accepts that important areas of care such as care in the community, psychological consequences of cancer, care of the patient facing death and aspects of pain control have not been included in the text of this book. The reasons for this are quite specific.

The management of pain in the cancer patient and relevant core care plans have been well described in the work of McCafferey and Bebe (1989). Care in the community and palliative care are areas of care that merit a book of their own, but this is not to suggest that much of the core care outlined in this manual will not be relevant to these client groups.

Psychological care for problems such as depression and the support and care of the individual facing recurrence of disease and, later, death fall primarily into the realms of individualised care, these areas of care have been omitted because they would often be too vague to be of any help, and they do not lend themselves readily to the development of core care plans. The giving of information as distinct from psychological support has been included because it is amenable to the development of a core care plan.

An argument could be advanced for the inclusion of surgical core care plans in this book, but such care plans would not be exclusive to cancer care. Are the core surgical problems faced (and consequent care given by the nurse) by a cancer patient undergoing stoma surgery for colonic cancer any different from a patient undergoing similar surgery for a diagnosis of ulcerative colitis? But, of course, the individual care would be exclusive to oncology. The core care required by a patient undergoing surgery for a brain tumour would not be greatly different from a patient undergoing surgery for trauma to the brain.

The requirement for a book such as this became evident through clinical practice. A variety of excellent textbooks exist detailing the care of cancer patients, often with care plans included, for example Tschudin (1988) and the series edited by Tiffany (1988, 1989). But there may be very little time to consult such texts in busy everyday clinical nursing practice.

This manual brings together the core care required by a great number of cancer patients in a readable and readily accessible manner. It forms a reference that can be consulted quickly in the often frantic clinical environment. It is recommended that it should be supported by reading conventional cancer nursing texts and a variety of research papers.

The Framework

To promote consistency and readability it is proposed that the framework for the core care plans should consist of four sections.

Section One	Proposed Treatment Intervention or Situation Requiring Nursing Intervention
Section Two	Common Potential Problems
Section Three	Nursing Intention
Section Four	Core Care

Section One. Identifies the proposed treatment or situation which may create a requirement by the patient for some manner of nursing intervention. The patient may have problems and concerns which will demand certain nursing actions to promote, for example his physical safety and psychological comfort.

Section Two. Highlights problems which require nursing intervention consequent to a specific treatment or situation. It is not intended to be an exhaustive list. Common problems are presented which the nurse could expect to encounter and be required to develop strategies for.

Section Three. Broad objectives are described which the nurse would hope to achieve while aiming for the promotion of safe and effective care. Individual outcomes in relation to the problems of a patient should be developed when planning care in conjunction with the patient, following assessment of his unique areas of need.

Section Four. Suggested points of which the nurse should be aware when providing the care and education of the patient. Brief descriptions of common points of care are given but would need to be developed further by the nurse for individual patients. A range of actions and interventions are outlined which make explicit the means by which the intent of the nurse is to be achieved. The provision of personalised health care is not exclusive to the nurse, and the involvement of other health care professionals at appropriate moments is acknowledged.

Core care plans are included for radiotherapy, chemotherapy and biotherapy and are supported by plans for bone marrow suppression, the oncology emergencies and various other problems which may result as a consequence of these cancer therapies.

Suggested readings accompany each plan or group of plans to encourage and enable nurses to utilise current nursing research, to ascertain relevance to their own clinical practice and rationale for care, if available. The author is influenced by the proposition that research must be at the heart of any nursing practice and the plans are influenced by that already available.

References

Clarke, M (1978) Planning nursing care: recent past, present and future *Nursing Times*, **74** (5) Occasional Paper, 17–20

Crow, R (1981) Research and standards of nursing care *Journal of Advanced Nursing*, (**6**) 491–496

Donabedian, A (1966) Evaluating the quality of medical care *Milbank Memorial Fund* Quarterly **64** (3), part 2, 166–206

Glasper, A, Stonehouse J, Martin, L (1987) Core Care Plans *Nursing Times*, **83** (10): 55–57

Grant, N (1975) The nursing care plan (2) *Nursing Times* **71** (13), occasional paper, 25–28

Hamilton-Smith, S (1972) *Nil By Mouth* London: Royal College of Nursing

Henderson, V (1973) On nursing care plans and their history *Nursing Outlook*, **21** (6): 378–379

Hurst, K (1985) Problem solving tests in nurse education *Nurse Education Today*, 5: 56–62

Kitson, A (1984) *Standards of Care: A Framework for Quality* London: Royal College of Nursing

Kitson, A (1989) *A Framework for Quality: A Patient Centred Approach to Quality Assurance in Health Care*. RCN Standards of Care Project London: Royal College of Nursing

Luthert, J (1990) *Assessing the Quality of Care in Cancer Nursing* A paper presented at the 5th Biennial (open) conference of the workgroup of European Nurse Researchers, September 5–7, Budapest, reported in the proceedings, pp 113–125

Luthert, J (1991) The Royal Marsden Hospital Standards of Care Project, Personal Communication

Luker, K (1984) An overview of evaluation research in nursing *Journal of Advanced Nursing*, **6**: 87–93

Martin, L and Glasper, A (1986) Core care plans: nursing models and the nursing process in action *Nursing Practice*, **1** (4): 268–273

McCaffery, M and Bebe, A (1989) *Pain, a Clinical Manual for Nursing Practice* St. Louis: C. V. Mosby

McFarlane, J and Casteldine, G (1982) *A Guide to the Practice of Nursing Using the Nursing Process* London: C. V. Mosby

Meyers, M (1972) *A Systematic Approach to the Nursing Care Plan* New York: Appleton-Century-Crofts

Nichols, E and Barstow, R (1980) Do nurses really use standard care plans? *Journal for Nursing Administration*, X (5), 27–31

Redfern, S and Norman, I (1990) Measuring the quality of nursing care: a consideration of alternative approaches *Journal of Advanced Nursing*, **15**: 1260–1272

Shea, H (1986) A conceptual framework to study the use of nursing care plans *International Journal of Nursing Studies*, **23** (2): 147–157

Tiffany, R and Pritchard, P eds (1988) *Oncology for Nurses and Health Care Professionals—Volume 1, Pathology Diagnosis and Treatment* London: Harper and Row

Tiffany, R and Webb, P (eds) (1988) *Oncology for Nurses and Health Care Professionals — Volume 2, Care and Treatment —* London: Harper and Row

Tiffany, R and Borky, D (eds) (1989) *Oncology for Nurses and Health Care Professionals – Volume 3, Cancer Nursing* London: Harper and Row

Tschudin, V (1988) *Nursing the Patient with Cancer* London: Prentice Hall

Wilson, C (1987) *Hospital Wide Quality Assurance* Toronto: W B Saunders

Wright, D (1984) An introduction to the evaluation of nursing care: a review of the literature *Journal of Advanced Nursing*, **9**: 457–467

Wright, L (1974) *Bowel Function in Hospital Patients* London: Royal College of Nursing

Wright, S (1987) Getting to the core of the matter, core care plans *Nursing Times*, **83** (24): 61–63

Wright, S (1990) *Building and Using a Model of Nursing*, London: Edward Arnold

---

Radiotherapy

INTRODUCTION

A large proportion of cancer patients are treated with some form of radiotherapy during the course of their illness. It is a well-established option in the cure, control and palliation of a variety of cancers in various sites of the body.

Frequently, patients will attend an out-patient department on a daily basis to receive radiotherapy and this has a number of implications for the nurse working in this environment. Patient assessment must aim to illuminate present knowledge about the disease and proposed treatment, the presence of anxieties and fears, educational ability and capacity for learning. It is paramount to establish a relationship within which the patient feels able to explore areas of concern and ask for reassurance and support.

The provision of appropriate education and information will hopefully alleviate misconceptions about radiotherapy, promote realistic expectations concerning treatment and facilitate patient anticipation of local and systemic side-effects. The ultimate goal is envisaged as the promotion of successful coping with both the physical and psychological sequelae of radiotherapy.

The achievement of such a goal by the nurse will not be possible in isolation; the contribution of the radiotherapist, therapeutic radiographer and other para-medical professionals in conjunction with the patient and his/her family must be examined when producing a plan of care.

Continuous monitoring and evaluation of the educational and informational interventions is acknowledged as vital. Measurement of how far a patient achieves proposed goals is necessary to facilitate effective care in the future.

As an example of brachytherapy (the administration of radiation in close proximity to the tumour), a core care plan detailing the care required by a patient undergoing treatment with iridium wires to the head and neck area is included. This is to draw attention to the diversity of radiotherapy, resulting in profoundly differing needs amongst patients. Intensive preparation and forward planning is necessitated to allow exploration of concepts of radiation safety, fears of isolation and myths concerning treatment.

Proposed Treatment Intervention

Cranial Radiotherapy

Common Potential Problems

Patchy alopecia, skin erythema, raised intracranial pressure, headache, nausea, dry mouth, bone marrow suppression, fatigue and lethargy.

Nursing Intention

1 The patient must be made aware of the potential side-effects and appropriate self-care measures.

2 The patient should experience minimal physical and psychological discomfort associated with the above.

Core Care

1 Provide pertinent verbal, written or audio-visual information about the nature of radiotherapy and its possible side-effects, outlining possible patient self-care measures.

2 Discuss the fact that hair may fall out after approximately 3 weeks and that there may only be partial regrowth. Refer the patient to the appliance officer for provision of a wig, if required, and suggest the use of scarves and turbans for women and caps for men.

3 Following consultation with the radiotherapist, advise the patient when washing the area exposed to radiation to splash it with tepid water and gently pat it dry with a soft towel. Advise not to use perfumed soap or cosmetics and only a gentle shampoo when washing hair, and to avoid direct sunlight. Men should use an electric shaver. Observe the skin regularly for any signs of skin irritation and/or breakdown.

4 Observe for any signs of raised intracranial pressure as indicated by alteration in the level of consciousness, projectile vomiting, headache, increased blood pressure and decreased pulse.

5 If the patient is nauseous, administer anti-emetics according to the pattern of nausea and monitor their effectiveness. Suggest other measures to help, such as sipping carbonated drinks, eating dry crackers, limiting sudden movements, relaxation and diversionary techniques.

6 If the patient's mouth becomes dry, encourage him to drink at least 2 l in 24 hours and eat moist food. Inspect his mouth daily for signs of soreness and infection. Use of a soft toothbrush and saline mouth washes four-hourly are advised to ensure comfort and adequate oral hygiene. Alert the patient who wears dentures to potential discomfort and to any care measures he will need to undertake.

7 Observe for any signs of bone marrow suppression.

8 If lethargic and easily fatigued, suggest that the patient should take frequent naps and limit his activity following treatment.

Proposed Treatment Intervention

Radiotherapy to the Head and Neck Area

Common Potential Problems

Mucositis, xerostomia, stomatitis leading to painful and difficult swallowing and predisposition to oral infection, skin erythema, hoarseness of voice and fatigue and lethargy.

Nursing Intention

1 The patient must be made aware of the potential side-effects and appropriate self-care measures.
2 The patient should experience minimal physical and psychological discomfort associated with the above.

Core Care

1 Provide pertinent verbal, written and audio-visual information about the nature of radiotherapy and its possible side-effects, outlining possible patient self-care measures.
2 Teach the patient how to assess the oral cavity each day for changes in mucosal integrity and signs of candida infection. Alert the patient who wears dentures to potential discomfort and to any care measures he will need to undertake.
3 Encourage the use of a soft toothbrush three times a day and rinsing of the mouth with saline after meals, to ensure comfort and adequate oral hygiene.
4 If the patient experiences any hoarseness of voice encourage him to limit talking as much as possible and avoid whispering, as this places strain on the voice.
5 The patient should avoid acidic and coarse textured foods, make use of sauces, oral liquid food supplements and moist soft food, sipping on liquids during meals to enable swallowing.
6 If necessary and prescribed, administer Mucaine gel or Xylocaine viscous prior to meals to alleviate pain and discomfort.
7 Lubricate the oral cavity with frequent sips of non-irritating fluid and/or artificial saliva if required.
8 Following consultation with the radiotherapist advise the patient when washing the area exposed to radiation to splash it with tepid water and gently pat it dry with a soft towel. Advise not to use perfumed soap, talc or cosmetics and to avoid direct sunlight. Observe the skin regularly for any signs of irritation and/or breakdown. Ask men to use an electric shaver.
9 Advise the patient to wear soft open-necked collars to prevent rubbing and possible damage to skin.
10 If the patient is lethargic and easily fatigued, suggest that the patient should take frequent naps and limit his activity following treatment.

Proposed Treatment Intervention

Oral Implant of Iridium-192

Common Potential Problems

Oral pain and discomfort, infection, local oedema resulting in difficult eating and breathing, alteration in oral sensation, impaired oral communication, fear, anxiety and isolation associated with radioactive sealed source and accidental radiation exposure to staff and visitors.

Nursing Intention

1 The patient must be aware of the procedure, possible sensations, appearance, side-effects and radiation precautions in addition to appropriate self-care measures.

2 The patient should experience minimal physical and psychological discomfort associated with the above.

3 To ensure a safe environment.

Core Care

1 Prior to insertion of iridium-192 provide pertinent verbal, written and audio-visual information regarding the nature of radiation, purpose and type of implant, implications of treatment, sensations to be expected and appropriate radiation protection measures.

2 Assessments of the patient's physical performance, oral and nutritional status will be necessary to predict expected nursing contact time. Opportunity to instruct the patient concerning oral care measures necessary to promote a clean and comfortable mouth should be taken.

3 Reassure the patient concerning fears of radiation and encourage him to verbalise concerns, providing explanations for limited contact time and isolation. Make the patient aware of measures to promote communications such as the telephone, intercom and picture cards and activities to pass the time.

4 Provide radiation protection in accordance with policy and procedure and with respect to the principles of time, distance and shielding. Ensure any visitors are aware of the necessity to enforce radiation protection precautions.

5 At regular intervals and at the beginning of each duty-change, identify the placement and position of wires. The oral cavity should be observed at this time to check for signs of infection, redness and swelling. Record and monitor the temperature daily or more often if indicated.

6 Ensure the patient performs oral care with a mouthwash containing saline or sodium bicarbonate. Encourage the patient to void the mouthwash into a plastic bowl rather then a wash-hand basin to ensure accidental dislodgement is recognised immediately.

7 Spicy and irritating foods should be omitted from the diet and a soft or liquid high protein diet may be preferable. Seek advice from dietitian if

required. Frequent drinks and ice lollies will provide moisture. Smoking and an intake of alcohol should be discouraged.

8   Assess the level of any pain and discomfort regularly. Consider the use of systemic analgesics and topical anaesthetics, and evaluate their effectiveness. Remind the patient that excessive verbal communication will probably enhance any discomfort.

9   Ensure the negotiated mechanisms for effective communication are available including paper and pencil and picture cards.

10 Ask the patient to report any difficulty in breathing or swallowing resulting from increased swelling. Ensure emergency suction and other emergency equipment are close by and in working order.

11 Steroids may be prescribed to reduce oedema. Encourage the patient to take tablets at mealtimes to prevent possible damage to the gastrointestinal mucosa, and with antacids if ordered. Monitor for signs of hyperglycaemia. The nurse should be aware of the possibility of:

- an increased appetite and weight gain
- retention of water
- mood changes
- lowered resistance to infection
- insomnia

Proposed Treatment Intervention

Radiotherapy to the Thoracic Cavity

Common Potential Problems
Skin erythema, oesophagitis, fatigue and lethargy, dry cough and bone marrow suppression.

Nursing Intention
1 The patient must be made aware of the potential side-effects and appropriate self-care measures.
2 The patient should experience minimal physical and psychological discomfort associated with the above.

Core Care
1 Provide pertinent verbal, written and audio-visual information about the nature of radiotherapy and its possible side-effects, outlining possible patient self-care measures.
2 Following consultation with the radiotherapist advise the patient when washing the area exposed to radiation to splash it with tepid water and gently pat it dry with a soft towel. Advise not to use perfumed soap and talc and to avoid direct sunlight. Observe the skin regularly for any signs of irritation and/or breakdown.
3 Advise the patient to wear soft, cotton non-constricting clothing. Women may need to avoid wearing a bra.
4 If lethargic and easily fatigued, suggest that the patient should take frequent naps and limit his activity following treatment.
5 Observe for any signs of bone marrow suppression.
6 Encourage the patient to drink cool fluids frequently, and administer cough linctus if prescribed, to soothe any cough.
7 If necessary and prescribed, administer Mucaine gel and/or Xylocaine viscous prior to meals to alleviate discomfort. Advise the patient to eat cool, soft and pureed foods and to drink plenty of cool liquids.

Proposed Treatment Intervention

Abdominal Radiotherapy

Common Potential Problems

Lethargy, bone marrow suppression, skin erythema, diarrhoea, nausea and anorexia.

Nursing Intention

1 The patient must be made aware of the potential side-effects and appropriate self-care measures.
2 The patient should experience minimal physical and psychological discomfort associated with the above.

Core Care

1 Provide pertinent verbal, written and audio-visual information about the nature of radiotherapy and its possible side-effects, outlining possible patient self-care measures.
2 If lethargic and easily fatigued, suggest that the patient should take frequent naps and limit his activity following treatment.
3 Observe for signs of bone marrow suppression.
4 Following consultation with the radiotherapist advise the patient when washing the area exposed to radiation to splash it with tepid water and gently pat it dry with a soft towel. Advise not to use perfumed soap and talc and to avoid direct sunlight. Observe the skin regularly for any signs of irritation and/or breakdown.
5 Advise the patient to wear soft, cotton non-constricting clothing.
6 If diarrhoea occurs, monitor the frequency, amount and appearance of any bowel motion. Ensure the perianal area is cleansed and dry following each bowel action. Maintain a record of intake and output. Encourage the patient to drink over 2 l in 24 h and in conjunction with the dietitian consider a low fat, low residue diet. Administer anti-diarrhoeal medication as prescribed and evaluate its effectiveness.
7 If the patient is nauseous, administer anti-emetics according to the pattern of nausea and monitor their effectiveness. Suggest other measures to help such as sipping carbonated drinks, eating dry crackers, limiting sudden movements, relaxation and diversionary techniques.
8 If the patient is anorexic, pay attention to the preparation and serving of meals, offer small and frequent meals that have a high protein and carbohydrate content and supplement with liquid nutritional supplements. Refer to the dietitian.
9 If bladder irritability occurs, ensure the patient is close to the toilet facilities, takes over 2 l of fluid in 24 h and observe the urine periodically for signs of infection.

CORE CARE PLAN 6

Proposed Treatment Intervention

Pelvic Radiotherapy

Common Potential Problems

Lethargy, bone marrow suppression, skin erythema, diarrhoea, nausea, anorexia, bladder irritability, vaginal discharge and alteration in sexual and reproductive function.

Nursing Intention

1 The patient must be made aware of the potential side-effects and appropriate self-care measures.
2 The patient should experience minimal physical and psychological discomfort associated with the above.

Core Care

1 Provide pertinent verbal, written and audio-visual information about the nature of radiotherapy and its possible side-effects, outlining possible patient self-care measures.
2 If lethargic and easily fatigued, suggest that the patient should take frequent naps and limit his activity following treatment.
3 Observe for any signs of bone marrow suppression.
4 Following consultation with the radiotherapist advise the patient when washing the area exposed to radiation to splash it with tepid water and gently pat it dry with a soft towel. Advise not to use perfumed soap or talc and to avoid direct sunlight. Observe the skin regularly for any signs of irritation and/or breakdown. Teach the patient about personal hygiene and provide sanitary pads for any vaginal discharge.
5 Advise the patient to wear soft, cotton non-constricting clothing.
6 If diarrhoea occurs, monitor the frequency, amount and appearance of any bowel motion. Ensure the patient's perianal area is cleansed and dry following each bowel action. Maintain a record of intake and output. Encourage the patient to drink over 2 l in 24 h and in conjunction with dietitian consider a low fat, low residue diet. Administer any anti-diarrhoeal medication as prescribed and evaluate its effectiveness.
7 If the patient is nauseous, administer anti-emetics according to the pattern of nausea and monitor effectiveness. Suggest other measures to help such as sipping carbonated drinks, eating dry crackers, limiting sudden movements, relaxation and diversionary techniques.
8 If the patient is anorexic, pay attention to the preparation and serving of meals. Offer small and frequent meals that have a high protein and carbohydrate content and supplement with liquid nutritional supplements. Refer to the dietitian.
9 Identify with the patient any potential problems regarding sexuality and reproductivity and allow opportunity for the discussion and exploration of feelings.

FURTHER READING

The following is a list of articles which provide an interesting and informative reference for the nurse involved in providing care for the patient undergoing radiotherapy.

Brandt, B (1989) What you should know about radiation implant therapy to the head and neck *Oncology Nursing Forum*, **16** (4): 579–582.

Campbell-Forsyth, L (1990) Patients' perceived knowledge and learning needs concerning radiation therapy. *Cancer Nursing* **13** (2): 81–89

Dudjak, L (1987) Mouth care for mucositis due to radiation therapy *Cancer Nursing*, **10** (3): 131–140

Eardley, A (1986) What do patients need to know? *Nursing Times*, **82** (16): 24–26

Hassey, K (1987) Radiation therapy for rectal cancer and the implications for nursing *Cancer Nursing*, **10** (6): 311–318

Hilderley, L (1983) Skin care in radiation therapy: A review of the literature *Oncology Nursing Forum* **10** (1): 51–56

Holmes, S (1981) Radiotherapy: Minimising the side-effects *The Professional Nurse*, **July**: 263–265

Huldi, A *et al* (1986) Alterations in taste appreciation in cancer patients during treatment *Cancer Nursing*, **9** (1): 38–41

Hussey, K (1985) Demystifying the care of patients with radioactive implants *American Journal of Nursing*, **85**: 789–792

Israel, M and Mood, D (1982) Three media presentations for patients receiving radiotherapy *Cancer Nursing*, **5** (1): 57–63

King, K *et al* (1985) Patients' descriptions of the experience of receiving radiation therapy *Oncology Nursing Forum*, **12** (4): 55–61

Kobashi-Schoot, J *et al* (1985) Assessment of malaise in cancer patients treated with radiotherapy *Cancer Nursing*, **8** (6): 306–313

Lewis, F (1988) Understanding radiotherapy *Cancer Nursing*, **11** (3): 174–185

Maddock, P (1987) Brachytherapy sources and applicators *Seminars in Oncology Nursing*, **3** (1): 15–22

Oncology Nursing Society Clinical Practice Committee (1982) Guidelines for nursing care of patients with altered protective mechanisms *Oncology Nursing Forum*, **9** (3), 114–118

Pritchard, A and David, J (eds) (1988) *Royal Marsden Hospital Manual of Clinical Nursing Procedures*. 2nd Edition London: Harper and Row

Royal Marsden Hospital (1985) *Radiotherapy. Your Questions Answered* Booklet

No. 2 produced by Patient Education Group Royal Marsden Hospital London

Strohl, A (1987) Head and neck implants *Seminars in Oncology Nursing*, **3** (1): 30–46

Welch, D (1980) Assessment of nausea and vomiting in cancer patients undergoing external beam radiotherapy *Cancer Nursing*, **3** (5): 365–371

Chemotherapy

INTRODUCTION

Chemotherapy is the use of drugs to destroy cancer cells with minimal toxicity to non-malignant cells. The goal of this systemic treatment may be to eliminate the disease or palliate metastatic disease, prolong survival and improve the quality of life. A rapidly expanding number of drugs is available and the process of learning about the individual differences is a challenge. Few other areas of nursing care demand as much knowledge about the treatment, skills in assessment, technical expertise and the ability and desire to support the patient emotionally, as does the nursing care of a patient undergoing chemotherapy.

Chemotherapy may be toxic in nature, possibly with life threatening consequences, and it is imperative for the nurse to be knowledgeable about the drugs and skilled in the care of those receiving them. Nurses involved in the preparation and administration of these drugs will encounter differing sorts of equipment and methods depending on the care environment and the institution. Correct procedures of preparation and administration should be strictly adhered to, protecting patients and staff, as outlined in local policy and procedure documentation. The scope of practice for an individual nurse varies within the areas cancer patients are cared for. Within the core care plans the assumption has been made that administration is carried out by the nurse; this is acknowledged as a specialist role.

Interventions suggested are within the realms of nursing practice and should be preceded by assessment and followed with sensitive evaluation. Care planning for the physiological and emotional aspects of care may be profitably undertaken as a partnership between patient and nurse, facilitating interventions which supplement and strengthen the patient's own behaviour. Close liaison between the pharmacist, doctor and other health care personnel is necessary to ensure patient safety and promote care of an excellent standard.

Teaching the patient and his/her family about the nature of treatment and its side-effects is paramount. Information may not be retained at first, and teaching and reinforcement should be a continuous process. Lack of recall may seriously impair the initiation of appropriate self-care behaviours in the hospital and home environment.

When reviewing the core care plans for patients undergoing chemotherapy it must be appreciated that only the commonly occurring problems have been identified, and the reader should refer to the literature for a full list of the expected side-effects and toxicities. The most commonly administered drugs, frequently given by the intravenous route, have been included, but the list is not intended to be exhaustive. It is acknowledged that some drugs are given by routes other than the intravenous route (for example intrathecally, intravesicularly and intracavitarily).

Proposed Treatment Intervention

Administration of Chemotherapy

Common Potential Problems

Lack of knowledge and anxiety concerning the procedures and side-effects associated with chemotherapy, nausea and vomiting, bone marrow suppression, fatigue, anorexia, alopecia and risk of extravasation and anaphylaxis (with certain drugs).

Nursing Intention

1 The patient will be physically and psychologically prepared prior to chemotherapy and be able to identify side-effects and appropriate self-care actions.

2 Problems associated with chemotherapy will be minimised.

3 Chemotherapy shall be given in an appropriate and safe manner.

Core Care

1 Review with the patient the possible side-effects which may occur during and following treatment and measures which the patient may use to minimise or alleviate them using verbal, written and audio-visual material. Opportunity should be given for exploration of issues important to the patient and where worries are evident.

2 Prior to administration be aware of the blood count and potential for bone marrow suppression, ensure the medical staff are aware of results which are not within normal parameters.

3 Administer the drugs and document the procedure according to prescription, protocol and hospital policy with due consideration given to sequence, timing and dose of drugs given. The administrator should be assured of the appropriate reconstitution and preparation of the drugs. Handle the drugs with respect and care, wearing a plastic apron and PVC or latex gloves and adhering to national and local policy guidelines.

4 If appropriate, administer prescribed anti-emetics 30 minutes prior to drug administration and at regular intervals thereafter. Monitor the effectiveness of these drugs and report to medical staff if vomiting is uncontrolled. Place a vomit bowl, tissues and mouthwash close to the patient and encourage him to use other additional measures to minimise nausea and vomiting such as sipping carbonated drinks, eating dry crackers, diversional and relaxation techniques and the removal of unpleasant odours, sights and sounds from the environment.

5 If appropriate, discuss with the patient the possibility of extravasation and/or anaphylaxis, in a sensitive manner, avoiding causing the patient any undue anxiety. Ensure the patient is aware of the importance of verbalising early signs of extravasation and/or anaphylaxis. Check that the appropriate emergency equipment is close to hand and ready for use.

6 Monitor the patient's appetite for any developing anorexia, offer dietary advice and a referral to the dietitian when appropriate.

7 Explain to the patient that he may feel tired and worn out at various times in between treatments. Encourage the patient to take frequent rest periods and naps and seek help with his daily activities where necessary.

8 If appropriate, discuss the occurrence of hair loss, and be aware of changes in body image and need for emotional support and practical advice.

Intravenous Bleomycin

Common Potential Problems

Tumour pain, fever and chills, skin reactions (erythema, prurituss, photosensitivity, hyperpigmentation and hyperkeritinisation) nail ridging and pulmonary changes.

Core Care

1 Prior to administration check any pulmonary function tests and baseline chest x-ray have been performed. Ensure the medical staff are aware of any abnormal results.

2 Administer any intravenous hydrocortisone cover as prescribed to abate fever and chills.

3 If tumour pain occurs, reassure the patient that the sensation will pass and administer a mild analgesic and evaluate its effectiveness.

4 In the event of fever and chills occurring, reassure the patient that symptoms will pass, cover him with warm blankets and record observations of temperature, pulse and blood pressure. Report to the medical staff if the readings are not within acceptable clinical limits. Be aware of potential for progressive anaphylaxis.

5 Assess the patient frequently on each admission for any impending pulmonary changes such as shortness of breath, cough, wheezing and exertional dyspnoea, and record and report any of the subtle changes.

6 Discuss the possible occurrence of an alteration in skin and nail appearance. Reassure the patient that the reaction will ususally subside, discuss the reason behind the occurrence and the necessity to avoid bright sunlight. Provide emotional support in the event of psychological reactions to alteration in his body image.

Intravenous Carboplatin

Common Potential Problems

Nausea and vomiting, bone marrow suppression, nephrotoxicity (less frequent than with cisplatin) and diarrhoea.

Core Care

1 Prior to administration check any renal function test results. Ensure the medical staff are aware of any abnormal results.

2 Make the patient aware of the importance of maintaining an oral intake if possible over 2 l in 24 hours, prior to and for 24 hours following completion of the infusion.

3 Record the patient's bowel action daily. Be aware of the potential for diarrhoea.

4 In the event of high dose carboplatin being administered be aware of probable bone marrow suppression (in particular thrombocytopenia) at 10–14 days post administration, and the need for close surveillance of blood counts and signs of infection and bleeding.

Intravenous Cisplatin

Common Potential Problems

Nausea and vomiting, diarrhoea, bone marrow suppression, metallic taste, renal toxicity, ototoxicity and neurotoxicity.

Core Care

1 Prior to administration check any renal function test results. Ensure the medical staff are aware of any abnormal results.

2 Ensure pre- and post-hydration are given according to the prescription and intake and output measured precisely during forced hydration. Administer any diuretics as prescribed and monitor their effectiveness. A daily weight estimation prior to breakfast should be recorded during hydration, and assess the patient for signs indicative of fluid and electrolyte imbalance.

3 Observe and determine the presence and severity of any paraesthesia, peripheral neuritis, tinnitus and high frequency hearing loss.

4 Record the patient's bowel action daily. Be aware of the potential for diarrhoea and constipation.

5 If a metallic taste occurs during the infusion, suggest the patient sucks a strongly flavoured sweet. Long-term taste changes should be assessed and dietary advice sought from dietitians. Suggest the patient uses a mouth wash prior to meals to refresh the palate.

Intravenous or Oral Cyclophosphamide

Common Potential Problems

Bone marrow suppression, alopecia, nausea and vomiting, mucositis, haemorrhagic cystitis, and a strange taste and facial flushing on administation.

Core Care

1 Prior to administration perform a urinalysis for blood. Ensure the medical staff are aware of any abnormal results.

2 Warn the patient he may experience a strange taste and some dizziness and flushing on intravenous administration. If these sensations occur ask him to suck a strongly flavoured sweet, and slow the rate of administration. Reassure patient the sensations will pass. Ensure the patient receives all oral dosages prescribed.

3 Consider the patient's hydrational status prior to and for up to 72 hours following administration. Encourage a fluid intake of 3 l in 24 hours. The drug should be administered in the morning to prevent urine collecting in the bladder overnight, and the patient should be encouraged to void urine frequently.

4 Ask the patient to observe and report any bloody urine or sensations of urgency or dysuria.

5 Teach the patient the importance of performing proper oral hygiene and a method of oral examination, stressing the importance of reporting any mouth soreness to a nurse or medical staff.

Intravenous Dacarbazine

Common Potential Problems

Severe nausea and vomiting, facial flushing during administration, flu-like syndrome and malaise, risk of extravasation, diarrhoea, pain during infusion and late bone marrow suppression.

Core Care

1 Photodegradation of dacarbazine is thought to contribute to venous pain during infusion and every effort should be made to protect the drug from light during reconstitution and infusion. Slowing administration may reduce discomfort. Be aware of the potential extravasation risk, continuously assessing for a sensation of discomfort during administration. Contact the medical officer and/or persons with responsibility for intravenous therapy immediately if any problems arise, and take appropriate action if extravasation occurs.

2 If facial flushing occurs, explain to the patient the transient nature of the symptom and slow the rate of administration. Advise the patient to avoid bright sunlight following administration.

3 In the event of a flu-like syndrome and malaise occurring, administer paracetamol as prescribed and monitor its effectiveness. Promote patient comfort and activity within his personal limits. Reassure the patient that the syndrome will only last for a short time.

4 Severe nausea and vomiting may occur (potentiated by photodegradation of the drug) but normally will improve on successive days of therapy.

5 Record the patient's bowel action daily. Be aware of the potential for diarrhoea.

6 Bone marrow suppression may occur at 2–4 weeks post-administration, ensure the patient is aware of probable side-effects and beneficial self-care measures.

Intravenous Doxorubicin

Common Potential Problems

Nausea and vomiting, stomatitis, alopecia, bone marrow suppression, facial flushing and vein streaking, risk of extravasation, cardiomyopathy and red discoloured urine.

Core Care

1 Prior to administration check any cardiac function tests. Ensure the medical staff are aware of any abnormal results.

2 Be aware of the potential extravasation risk, continuously assessing for a sensation of discomfort during administration. Contact the medical officer and/or persons with responsibility for intravenous therapy immediately if any problems arise, and take appropriate action if extravasation occurs.

3 If facial flushing and vein streaking occur, explain to the patient the transient nature of these symptoms, and slow the rate of administration.

4 Monitor the patient for signs of congestive heart failure and changes in pulse quality, rate and rhythm.

5 Teach the patient the importance of the performance of proper oral hygiene and a method of oral examination, stressing the importance of reporting any mouth soreness to a nurse or medical staff.

6 Inform the patient of possible changes in the colour of his urine for 24 hours following chemotherapy and that this is of no cause for concern and has no detrimental effects.

Intravenous Etoposide

Common Potential Problems

Severe hypotension if infused in less than 30 minutes, mild nausea and vomiting, alopecia and bone marrow suppression.

Core Care

Be aware of possibility of hypotension occurring, if etoposide is infused in less than 30 minutes, monitor the infusion rate closely. Ask the patient to report any light-headedness or dizziness, and advise him to take his time when changing position and rising from the bed or chair.

Intravenous 5-Fluorouracil

Common Potential Problems

Diarrhoea, mild nausea, stomatitis, bone marrow suppression, darkening of veins used for infusion and hyperpigmentation.

Core Care

1 Teach the patient the importance of proper oral hygiene and a method of oral examination, stressing the importance of reporting any mouth soreness to a nurse or medical staff.

2 Record the patient's bowel action daily. Be aware of the potential for diarrhoea.

3 Discuss with the patient the possible occurrence of changes in vein and skin appearance. Reassure him the reaction will subside, and the reason behind the occurrence of such changes and the necessity to avoid bright sunlight. Provide the patient with emotional support in the event of psychological reactions to an alteration in body image.

Intravenous High Dose Cytosine Arabinoside

Common Potential Problems

Severe bone marrow suppression, stomatitis, nausea and vomiting, hyperuricaemia, diarrhoea and abdominal cramps, conjunctivitis, flu-like syndrome, cutaneous changes, hepatotoxicity, neurotoxicity and alopecia.

Core Care

1   Prior to administration check any renal and liver function tests. Ensure the medical staff are aware of any abnormal results.

2   Teach the patient the importance of the performance of proper oral hygiene and a method of oral examination, stressing the importance of reporting any mouth soreness or signs of candida infection to a nurse or medical staff. Oral hygiene should be carried out with the prescribed prophylactic oral antifungal agents and mouth wash solutions at appropriate times.

3   Bone marrow suppression may be severe, monitor the blood count for the approaching nadir at 7–14 days post-administration. Implement appropriate care concerning the potential risks of infection, bleeding and anaemia.

4   Ensure two-hourly steroid eye drops are administered as prophylaxis against conjunctivitis on commencement of therapy and for one week following cessation of therapy, if prescribed. Ask the patient to report any discomfort or photophobia and to observe for any redness.

5   Monitor the condition of the patient's skin regularly for any evidence of flaking or erythema particularly on the palms and soles of the feet. Instruct the patient to avoid alcohol-based skin products and to use emollient creams.

6   Monitor the patient for signs of a disruption in liver function as evidenced by jaundice, fatigue, anorexia and a deviation of liver function tests from the normal.

7   Fever and flu-like syndrome may occur; in the event of such, monitor the patient's temperature, administer paracetamol if prescribed and evaluate its effectiveness. In addition provide the patient with appropriate comfort measures. Reassure the patient that his symptoms will subside.

8   Record the patient's bowel action daily. Be aware of the potential for diarrhoea. In the event of the patient experiencing abdominal cramping, provide heat packs and avoid the administration of opiate analgesics which may potentiate paralytic ileus.

9   Administer allopurinol to the patient as prescribed. Ensure a fluid intake of over 2 l in 24 hours and maintain a precise record of intake and output, and evaluate the patient for any signs of renal insufficiency.

10 Monitor the patient's neurological status and report any untoward symptoms such as confusion, headache, ataxia and somnolence immediately.

Intravenous High Dose Methotrexate

Common Potential Problems

Stomach, gut and oral ulceration, hyperuricaemia, nausea and vomiting, bone marrow suppression, nephrotoxicity and a maculopapular rash.

Core Care

1 Record the patient's intake and output and monitor his renal function. Renal failure is most likely to occur 24 h following therapy. Administer sodium bicarbonate in hydration intravenously according to prescription, usually alternating 1 l of dextrose with 1 l of saline +70 mmols of potassium chloride and 70 mmols of sodium bicarbonate, every four hours. The patient's urine output should be maintained at a rate of 100 ml/h with a pH value above 8 prior to the administration of the prescribed methotrexate, and during the post-hydration period. If the value is not maintained at or above 8, further hydration and alkalinisation should take place, on consultation with the medical officer.

2 Ensure blood is taken in order to estimate methotrexate levels normally 4 h, 24 h, 48 h, and 72 h post administration. Ensure the medical staff are aware of the results. Administer prescribed folinic acid at 24 h post-methotrexate administration, intravenously, normally for 10 doses, at an interval of every 6 h.

3 Administer allopurinol as prescribed and ensure the patient's oral intake of 2 l in 24 hours is maintained.

4 Teach the patient the importance of the performance of proper oral hygiene and a method of oral examination, stressing the importance of reporting any mouth soreness to a nurse or medical staff.

5 Note the patient's bowel actions and report any extensive diarrhoea.

6 Make the patient aware of the importance of the appearance of any maculopapular rash (usually occurring one week later) as this normally heralds impending renal failure, stomatitis and bone marrow suppression.

Intravenous High Dose Melphalan

Common Potential Problems
Renal toxicity with fluid and electrolyte imbalance potentiated by nausea and vomiting, diarrhoea and a forced diuresis, alopecia, stomatitis, bone marrow suppression and depressive mood changes.

Core Care
1 Prior to administration check any renal function tests. Ensure the medical staff are aware of any abnormal results.

2 Commence intravenous hydration and maintain a strict record of intake and output at hourly intervals (the patient will usually have a urinary catheter inserted). Intravenous frusemide will be given as prescribed to achieve a diuresis of 200 ml of urine every 10 minutes in the half hour prior to administration of melphalan.

3 Following administration maintain a diuresis of 200 ml of urine every 10 minutes for a period of one hour and then 500 ml of urine per hour for a further four hours.

4 Baseline central venous pressure recordings may be obtained and then recorded hourly for three hours, continuing if the patient's clinical condition indicates it. Monitor the patient's hydration status on a continuous basis and inform the medical staff if his condition is indicative of dehydration or circulatory overload.

5 Maintain a precise record of intake and output, and weigh the patient daily at the same hour each day. Monitor for any signs which may indicate a developing renal dysfunction.

6 Record the patient's bowel action daily. Be aware of the potential for diarrhoea.

7 Teach the patient the importance of the performance of proper oral hygiene and a method of oral examination, stressing the importance of reporting any mouth soreness or signs of candida infection to a nurse or medical staff. Oral hygiene should be carried out with the prescribed prophylactic oral antifungal agents and mouthwash solutions at appropriate times.

8 Bone marrow suppression may be delayed and prolonged, 14–30 days post-administration. Ensure any prescribed prophylactic intravenous antibiotics are commenced at the appropriate time and monitor the patient's blood count for the approaching nadir. Implement appropriate care for the potential risks of infection, bleeding and anaemia.

9 Monitor the patient's emotional feelings and for the development of possible depression. Allow him time to express his feelings and opportunities for discussion of any perceived problems. Ensure activities are available to alleviate the patient's boredom.

Intravenous Ifosfamide

Common Potential Problems

Bone marrow suppression, nausea and vomiting, cerebral encephalopathy, haemorrhagic cystitis, renal toxicity and inappropriate anti-diuretic hormone secretion.

Core Care

1 Prior to administration check any renal function test results and perform a routine ward urinalysis. Ensure the medical staff are aware of any abnormal results.

2 Ensure pre- and post-hydration are given according to the prescription, and record intake and output precisely. If the urine output falls to below 100 ml/hour administer frusemide as ordered and monitor its effectiveness. A daily weight prior to breakfast should be estimated during hydration and assess the patient for signs indicative of fluid retention.

3 Ensure mesna is administered at the appropriate times and dose, to counteract the effects of ifosfamide on the bladder wall, possibly leading to haematuria.

4 Encourage the patient to empty his bladder at frequent intervals and to take fluids in excess of 2 l in 24 hours. Urine should be tested each time the patient voids and a particular note made of the presence of blood and protein. Ketones are to be expected with mesna rescue. Ascertain if the patient has any discomfort when passing urine.

5 Administer dexamethasone as prescribed and monitor for any changes in the patient's level of consciousness. Record pulse and blood pressure four hourly and report any subtle changes. Avoid the use of lorazepam as an anti-emetic if at all possible as this will mask changes in the patient's neurological status.

Intravenous Methotrexate

Common Potential Problems
Bone marrow suppression, nausea, stomatitis and skin reactions (erythematous rash, pruritus and photosensitivity).

Core Care
1 Teach the patient the importance of the performance of proper oral hygiene and a method of oral examination, stressing the importance of reporting any mouth soreness to a nurse or medical staff. Ensure folinic acid rescue is given when the dose or condition of the patient warrants administration, intravenously or orally as prescribed. If the patient is unable to tolerate oral doses inform the medical staff. Ensure all doses are given at correct times.

2 Explain the reason for any skin changes or photosensitivity which develop. Reassure the patient that the effect is temporary. Provide the patient with symptomatic treatment and advise him to refrain from exposure to bright sunlight.

Intravenous Mitomycin C

Common Potential Problems
Nausea and vomiting, risk of extravasation, stomatitis, alopecia, delayed and prolonged bone marrow suppression, and nephrotoxicity in cumulative doses.

Core Care
1 Prior to administration check any renal function tests. Ensure the medical staff are aware of any abnormal results.

2 Be aware of potential extravasation risk. Assess continuously for a sensation of discomfort during administration and contact the medical officer and/or persons with responsibility for intravenous therapy immediately if any problems arise, and take appropriate action if extravasation occurs.

3 Teach the patient the importance of the performance of proper oral hygiene and a method of oral examination, stressing the importance of reporting any mouth soreness to a nurse or medical staff.

4 Bone marrow suppression may be delayed and prolonged 4–8 weeks post-administration, ensure the patient is aware of probable side-effects and beneficial self-care measures.

5 Monitor the patient's fluid intake and output precisely during treatment and ensure prescribed hydration is administered at the appropriate time and at the correct rate.

Intravenous Mitozantrone

Common Potential Problems

Mild nausea and vomiting, anorexia, green discoloured urine, minimal alopecia, bone marrow suppression and cardiotoxicity (increased risk with previous chest irradiation and cardiovascular disease).

Core Care

1 Prior to administration check any cardiac function tests. Ensure medical staff are aware of any abnormal results.

2 Monitor the patient for signs of congestive heart failure and changes in pulse quality, rate and rhythm.

3 Inform the patient of possible changes in the colour of his urine for 24 hours following chemotherapy, and that this is no cause for concern and has no detrimental effects.

Intravenous or Oral Steroids

Common Potential Problems

Increase in weight due to fluid retention and fat deposits, insomnia, mood changes, stomach irritation and ulcers, hypertension, acne, diabetes mellitus, increased appetite and problems associated with abrupt withdrawal of therapy.

Core Care

1 When administering oral steroids try to give tablets with meals to help avoid damage to the gastrointestinal mucosa, and with antacids if ordered.

2 If possible avoid administration of the drug in the evening, as steroids may exacerbate insomnia. Encourage the patient to perform actions which have been found helpful to promote sleep in the past.

3 Weigh the patient daily, and be aware of possibility of fluid retention, fat deposits and an increased appetite leading to weight gain. Observe for any puffiness in the patient's ankles and hands and encourage him to elevate his feet as much as possible.

4 Weight gain, acne and mood changes may lead to disturbances in the patient's body image. Allow him the opportunity to express his feelings and reassure him the effects will subside on discontinuing therapy. Consider a dietetic referral.

5 Monitor the patient's blood pressure on a regular basis for trends indicative of hypertension, and report any changes to the medical officer.

6 Monitor the patient for signs of diabetes mellitus and perform a daily urinalysis for glucose and acetone.

7 Assess the patient for any mood changes which could herald the beginning of a steroid-induced dementia or psychosis. Explain the occurrence of any depression or agitation to the patient and his significant others and provide them with appropriate emotional support.

8 Be aware of an increased susceptibility to infection, and educate the patient accordingly.

9 Impress upon the patient the importance of taking tablets at prescribed times when at home and not to suspend medication abruptly, and to carry a card indicating the bearer is receiving steroid therapy.

Intravenous Vincristine

Common Potential Problems
Constipation, numbness, tingling and paraesthesia in hands and feet and a risk of extravasation.

Core Care
1 Be aware of the potential extravasation risk. Assess continuously for a sensation of discomfort during administration and contact the medical officer and/or persons with responsibility for intravenous therapy immediately if any problems arise, and take appropriate action if extravasation occurs.
2 Warn of the possibility of constipation occurring, suggest the patient takes a high fibre diet, an increased fluid intake and regular exercise. If the patient is prone to constipation, employ the use of prophylactic aperients when prescribed, and monitor the bowel action daily.
3 Observe and determine the severity of any change in the sensations of the hands and feet. Reassure the patient the symptoms will subside in the 6–8 weeks following the cessation of treatment. Educate the patient concerning the prevention of injury to numb hands and feet, avoiding extremes of temperature and modifying the environment. Evaluate any changes in sensation prior to each treatment and inform the medical officer.

Further Reading

The following is a list of references where the nurse caring for the patient undergoing chemotherapy will find useful sources of information to facilitate the provision of safe and competent nursing care.

Conrad, K J (1986) Cerebellar toxicities associated with cytosine arabinoside: A nursing perspective *Oncology Nursing Forum*, **13** (5): 57–79

David, J and Speechley, V (1987) Scalp cooling to prevent alopecia *Nursing Times*, **83** (32): 36–37

Dodd, M J and Mood, D W (1981) Chemotherapy: Helping patients to know the drugs they are receiving and their side effects *Cancer Nursing*, **14** (4): 311–318

Engleking, C H and Steele, N E (1984) A model for pretreatment nursing assessment of patients receiving cancer chemotherapy *Cancer Nursing*, **7** (3): 203–212

Eustace, P (1980) History and development of cisplatinum in the management of malignant disease *Cancer Nursing*, **3** (5): 373–378

Horder, L and Hatfield, A (1982) Patient participation in monitoring myelosuppression from chemotherapy *Oncology Nursing Forum*, **9** (2): 35–37

FURTHER READING

Kaszyk, L K (1986) Cardiac toxicity associated with cancer therapy *Oncology Nursing Forum*, **13** (4): 81–88

Kennedy, M *et al* (1981) Chemotherapy related nausea and vomiting: A survey to identify problems and interventions *Oncology Nursing Forum*, **8** (1): 19–22

Levid, J and Bush, J (1987) Nurses' role in chemotherapy administration *Seminars In Oncology Nursing*, **3** (2): 83–86

Lerman, C, Rimer, B, Blumberg, B *et al* (1990) Effects of coping style and relaxation on cancer chemotherapy side effects and emotional responses. *Cancer Nursing*, **13** (5): 308–315

Lyndon, J (1986) Nephrotoxicity of cancer treatment *Oncology Nursing Forum*, **13** (2): 68–77

Marino, E B and LeBlanc, D H (1975) Cancer chemotherapy *Nursing*, **75**, November: 22–33

Miller, S A (1980) Nursing action in cancer chemotherapy administration *Oncology Nursing Forum*, **7** (4): 8–16

Royal College of Nursing (1989) *Safe Practice with Cytotoxics* London: Royal College of Nursing

Royal Marsden Hospital (1985) *Chemotherapy. Your Questions Answered* Booklet No. 1 Produced By The Patient Education Group, Royal Marsden Hospital, London

Scogna, D M and Smalley, R V (1979) Chemotherapy induced nausea and vomiting *American Journal of Nursing*, **September:** 1562–1564

Swatz, A and Ellington, O (1978) Cisplatinum – A brief review of its uses and nursing guidelines *Cancer Nursing*, **1** (5): 403–405

Tierney, A J (1987) Preventing chemotherapy induced alopecia in cancer patients: Is scalp cooling worthwhile? *Journal of Advanced Nursing*, **12**: 303–310

Todres, R and Wojtiuk, R (1979) The cancer patient's view of chemotherapy *Cancer Nursing*, **12** (4): 283–286

Trester, A K (1982) Nursing management of patients receiving cancer chemotherapy *Cancer Nursing*, **5** (3): 201–210

Warren, K (1988) Will I be sick nurse? Part 1 and Part 2 *Nursing Times*, **84** (11): 30–31 *Nursing Times*, **84** (12): 30–31

Wickham, R (1986) Pulmonary toxicity secondary to cancer treatment *Oncology Nursing Forum*, **13** (5): 69–76

Biological Therapies

INTRODUCTION

Biological therapy is not currently considered a standard cancer therapy, but research activity is at present focused upon determining the contribution of the biologicals and biological response modifiers.

Biological response modifiers are those agents or approaches that modify the relationship between tumour and host by modifying the host's biological response to the tumour with a resultant therapeutic effect. A number of substances, including interferons, monoclonal antibodies, tumour necrosis factor, interleukins and colony stimulating factors, has been identified as holding a potential role in the treatment of cancer. The anti-tumour effects of interferons have been documented with particular reference to hairy cell leukaemia, melanoma and Kaposi's sarcoma. Specific cancers refractory to other forms of therapy have demonstrated some response to interleukin 2 (such as metastatic melanoma and renal cell carcinoma).

The increasing use of such approaches prompts a call for nurses caring for cancer patients to be conversant with the biological and immunological bases of these therapies. This is necessary with a particular reference to the establishment and standardisation of procedures for monitoring side-effects.

The toxicities observed while caring for this patient population are distinct from those seen with chemotherapy. Toxicities tend to be more complex, subjective in nature and hence difficult to assess. Nurses must be prepared to plan care relevant to the clinical uses, unique to this form of therapy. Patients fully informed about the possible side-effects will be placed in an ideal situation to inform nurses of subtle changes in their subjective state.

Diverse physiological and acute and chronic constitutional symptoms may present in a patient receiving a biological response modifier. Each agent or approach used clinically is associated with a few of its own toxicities, there are some commonalities which can be identified and these are described in the core care plan. The variety and frequency with which they occur along with the severity vary immensely and clarification should be sought in the growing body of literature.

Nursing research studies are urgently needed to address methods of quantifying side-effects such as malaise and flu-like syndrome, followed by investigation of methods to prevent and control them.

Extensive media coverage of various forms of biological therapy may have influenced patients and their families producing unrealistic expectations of cure. Informed consent is vital; not denying patient's hope, but tempered realistically. A core care plan is presented which outlines the pertinent issues faced by patients undergoing investigative therapy. A patient requiring an investigative agent of any kind requires informative support from knowledgeable and caring staff.

CORE CARE PLAN   25

Proposed Treatment Intervention

Biological Therapies

The patient is to receive a biological response modifier.

Common Potential Problems

Anxiety and anticipation associated with the use of an investigational therapy, lack of feelings of control over persistent side-effects which may include: fatigue, malaise, fever, rigors, headache, dry skin, erythema, pruritus, nausea and vomiting, anorexia, diarrhoea, alteration in neurological status (somnolence, mood alteration and confusion), alteration in cardiovascular status (hypo- or hypertension, arrythmias, capillary leak syndrome with interleukin therapy leading to pulmonary oedema, dyspnoea, weight gain and fluid imbalance), alteration in renal function (proteinuria and oliguria and changes in creatinine and electrolytes levels) and alteration in liver function (elevated liver function tests) and alteration in haematological status (neutropenia, thrombocytopenia, anaemia and coagulopathies).

Nursing Intention

1 The patient will be physically and psychologically prepared prior to receiving therapy. Information and support must be provided to enable the patient to identify and monitor side-effects, initiate self-care measures and maintain feelings of control.

2 Problems associated with therapy will be minimised or alleviated.

3 Therapy will be given in an appropriate and safe manner.

Core Care

1 Prior to therapy review with the patient his understanding and knowledge concerning the immune system, the particular therapy to be employed and the treatment plan. Outline in detail the possible side-effects which may occur during and following treatment, self-monitoring techniques and self-care measures which the patient may use to minimise or alleviate symptoms. Written and audio-visual material should be made available.

2 Ensure all baseline observations and blood tests are performed prior to therapy and the results made known to the medical staff.

3 Administer the therapy according to the prescription and following consultation with the research protocol. Familiarity with the type of therapy, route of administration and drug schedule should be ensured.

4 Following an initial thorough assessment of the patient perform regular and consistent monitoring, reporting subtle changes in:
   - pulse-record rate, rhythm and characteristics
   - respirations – record the rate and rhythm and any onset of dyspnoea
   - blood pressure – remain vigilant for possible hypo- or hypertension. Patients experiencing a drop in blood pressure of 10 mm/Hg with symptoms, or 20 mm/Hg without symptoms may require supportive intravenous therapy if necessary

---

Biological therapies

- temperature – record temperature and the occurrence of any rigors. Monitor the patient for signs of infection. During a fever institute measures to promote comfort and lower temperature which may include fanning, tepid sponging and the provision of a well-ventilated environment. Provide extra blankets in the event of a rigor and offer support and reassurance to the patient. Consider with the patient the use of relaxation techniques, biofeedback and imagery. If prescribed, ensure the patient receives premedication and regular doses of a non-steroidal anti-inflammatory agent or a narcotic analgesic to minimise rigors. Evaluate the effectiveness of any interventions.
- neurological status – ask family members to report any subtle changes in mood, presence of confusion or somnolence. Ensure the patient is aware that depression may persist for some time after finishing therapy. Consider the possibility of drug-induced changes in neurological condition.
- fluid balance – maintain a precise account of intake and output and weigh daily at breakfast time. Maintain an awareness for the possibility of and signs indicating circulatory overload and a deteriorating renal function. Perform a urinalysis daily and report the presence of blood and protein.

5 If the patient experiences a headache and/or myalgias, administer paracetamol if prescribed and evaluate its effectiveness. Provide a quiet environment and suggest to the patient the use of cool compresses to his head and limbs, massage and relaxation techniques.

6 In the event of itching, dry skin and a rash, consider the use of antihistamine therapy. Evaluate the effectiveness of the drug following administration.

7 In the event of fatigue, consider strategies in conjunction with the patient and the occupational therapist which may promote energy conservation, effective energy utilisation and energy restoration. It may be helpful to:
- prioritise and pace activities, considering alternative ways to accomplish activities of daily living
- alter patterns of activity and rest and times for sleeping and waking
- employ relaxation and distraction strategies
- pay attention to factors such as nutrition, social needs, environmental conditions and the presence of other symptoms.

8 Interventions known to be helpful in reducing anorexia, nausea and vomiting and diarrhoea during conventional therapies should be explored if necessary. Consider a referral to the dietitian.

9 Be aware of the potential for changes in biochemical and haematological status.

10 Provide the patient with opportunities for the examination of anxieties and feelings of anticipation over the use of an investigative treatment. Explore

with the patient any unrealistic expectation of treatment and care if appropriate. Provide information and support (particularly about what is happening) and the expected outcome of interventions, to enhance coping and promote feelings of control.

Further Reading

Abernathy, E (1987) Biotherapy: An overview *Oncology Nursing Forum*, **14** (6), Supplement: 13–15

Brogley, J and Sharpe, E (1990) Nursing care of patients receiving activated lymphocytes *Oncology Nursing Forum*, **17** (2): 187–196

Gallucci, B (1987) The immune system and cancer *Oncology Nursing Forum*, **14** (6), Supplement: 3–12

Garvey, E *et al* (1983) Care of the patient undergoing interferon therapy *Cancer Nursing*, **6** (4): 303–306

Glaspy, J and Ambersley, J (1990) The promise of colony stimulating factors in clinical practice *Oncology Nursing Forum*, **16** (6), Supplement: 20–24

Haebur, D (1989) Recent advances in the management of biotherapy related side effects – flu like syndrome *Oncology Nursing Forum*, **16** (2): 247–255

Lind, M (1980) The immunological assessment: A nursing focus *Heart and Lung*, **9** (4): 658–661

Mayer, D and Schoenberger, C (1982) Biological response modifiers *Oncology Nursing Forum*, **9** (1): 45–49

Parkinson, D (1988) Interleukin 2 in cancer therapy *Seminars in Oncology*, **16** (6) Supplement: 10–26

Piper, B *et al* (1989) Recent advances in the management of biotherapy related side effects – fatigue *Oncology Nursing Forum*, **16** (6) Supplement: 27–34

Strauman, J (1988) The nurse's role in the biotherapy of cancer: Nursing research of the side effects *Oncology Nursing Forum*, **15** (6), Supplement: 35–39

Suppers, J and McClamrock, E (1985) Biologicals in cancer treatment: Future effects on nursing practice *Oncology Nursing Forum*, **12** (3): 27–32

Oueseda, J *et al* (1986) Clinical toxicity of interferons in cancer patients: A review *Journal of Clinical Oncology*, **4** (2): 234–243

The reader's attention is particularly drawn to supplements produced by *Oncology Nursing Forum* entitled The biotherapy of cancer. *Oncology Nursing Forum* 14 (6) (1987), 15 (6) (1988) and 16 (6) (1989).

Situation Requiring Nursing Intervention

Informed Consent and Clinical Trials

The patient is to make a decision regarding treatment with an investigational agent.

Potential Problems

Lack of information concerning the proposed treatment, purpose, method, benefits, risks, uncertainties and available alternative treatment, the incidence, severity, seriousness and management of possible side-effects leading to an inability to make an informed decision regarding treatment and in the event of acceptance, inability to care for oneself.

Nursing Intention

1 To act as the patient's advocate during the process of informed consent.

2 To ensure appropriate information is provided which the patient understands and allows appropriate self-management during and following treatment.

Core Care

1 Ensure the current protocol and literature are available within the clinicl area to enable nurses to update their knowledge concerning the protocol, known or potential toxicities and symptom management.

2 To enable the patient to make an informed decision regarding treatment, it should be ensured that oral and written explanations are made available concerning the:
   - format of the study
   - any procedures to be followed and purposes of such procedures
   - identification of likely physical risks and discomforts
   - outline of expected benefits
   - measures to ensure confidentiality and anonymity
   - freedom to withdraw from the study without jeopardising any future treatment and care
   - responsibilities of the patient such as clinic and in patient attendance, documentation and reporting side-effects.

The explanations made should be simple and concise and in a language the patient comprehends.

3 To enable appropriate education and the identification of any knowledge deficit an assessment of the knowledge of the disease, medical management, content of informed consent and educational ability (capacity to learn, level of anxiety and ability to take decisions) will be necessary.

4 Appropriate strategies to facilitate learning should be utilised to complement and consolidate information given by medical colleagues.

5 The nurse should be satisfied that the protocol has been presented, considered and approved by the appropriate ethical committee.

6 If necessary, the nurse may be called upon to witness the signing of consent form. The witness should be able to ask salient questions concerning details

of the study, feeling comfortable that the patient understands the central issues.

During treatment:

7 Informed consent is a continuous process, it should be ensured that learning needs are continually assessed, information provided, questions answered and concerns addressed.

8 Carefully observe and document in the care plan, and any other necessary documents, the clinical consequences of treatment, thus facilitating rapid attention to any adverse side-effects, and thorough evaluation of the treatment protocol.

9 Remain in close contact with all members of the research team to allow dissemination of relevant information and co-ordination of care needs.

10 Provide support to any patient who wishes to withdraw from the study for whatever reason, allaying and exploring such feelings of guilt, disappointment and fears for future treatment.

Further Reading

Cassileth, B et al (1980) Informed consent – why are its goals imperfectly realised? New England Journal of Medicine, 302: 896–900

Chamoroo, T and Applebaum, J (1988) Informed consent: Nursing issues and ethical dilemmas Oncology Nursing Forum, 15 (6): 803–808

Cogliano-Shitta, N (1986) Paediatric Phase 1 trials: Ethical issues and nursing considerations Oncology Nursing Forum, 13 (2): 29–32

Gross, J (1986) Clinical research in cancer chemotherapy Oncology Nursing Forum, 13 (1): 59–65

Jassak, P and Ryan, M (1989) Ethical issues in clinical research Seminars in Oncology Nursing, 5 (2): 102–108

Karan, D and Wiltshaw, E (1986) How well informed? Cancer Nursing, 9 (5): 238–242

Melia, K (1989) Everyday Nursing Ethics London: Churchill Livingstone

Rimer, B et al (1984) Informed consent: A crucial step in cancer patient education Health Education Quarterly, 10: 30

Royal College of Nursing (1977) Ethics related to research in nursing: Guidance for nurses involved in research, or any study/project concerning human subjects London: Royal College of Nursing

Varrichio, C and Jassak, P (1989) Informed consent: An overview Seminars in Oncology Nursing, 5 (2): 95–98

Bone Marrow Suppression

INTRODUCTION

All nurses caring for cancer patients will at one time or another be confronted in the clinical situation with patients experiencing episodes of bone marrow suppression, resulting from the disease process or the treatment strategies. Intensive chemotherapy and radiotherapy protocols are placing many more patients at risk of developing anaemia, thrombocytopenia and neutropenia.

It is recognised that the nurse can play a key role in utilising swift, accurate assessments and appropriate interventional skills, to reduce the significant morbidity and mortality associated with this phenomenon. Central to the performance of this role is a detailed understanding of the underlying concepts of how bone marrow and blood cells function.

Monitoring for subtle changes in the patient's physical and psychological status is essential to facilitate early detection of potentially life threatening events. Any small deviation from the normal will only be recognised following an intelligent assessment of the integument and the cardiovascular, immune and haematopoietic systems. The frequency of continued assessments will be determined following consideration of the individual patient.

Successful prevention, detection and management strategies are only possible in close co-operation with the patient. The patient must realise the importance of self-monitoring and self-care techniques. Following individual teaching programmes an appreciation of self-responsibility may neutralise any previous feeling of loss of control and foster feelings of an intimate involvement in care.

Situation Requiring Nursing Intervention

Potential Bone Marrow Suppression

Suppression due to treatment or the disease process.

Common Potential Problems
Infection, bleeding and anaemia.

Nursing Intention
1 The at risk patient will be made aware of the potential problems associated with the above and be able to recognise the early signs and symptoms.

2 Bone marrow suppression will be detected early before serious effects ensue.

Core Care
1 Following a thorough assessment identify the patient at risk and provide appropriate information and education to him concerning the early signs of:
   - infection – chills, a flushed appearance, fever and feeling generally unwell and any pain, swelling or tenderness over the skin
   - bleeding – easy bruising, nose bleeds, petechiae, haematuria and conjunctival haemorrhages
   - anaemia – lethargy and fatigue, headache, dizziness and breathlessness. Emphasise the necessity for the patient to monitor and report to medical staff immediately when initial signs and symptoms occur.

2 In conjunction with the medical staff ensure a regular full blood count is performed and the results reviewed.

3 Teach the patient how to perform oral hygiene prior to and following meals and to inspect his mouth for signs indicative of a fungal infection.

4 Observations of temperature, pulse and blood pressure may be monitored four hourly and subtle changes should be reported to the medical staff, which may indicate signs of infection or bleeding.

5 Ensure as far as possible that the patient maintains a safe environment free from exogenous sources of infection, potential trauma and accidents, for example, paying attention to meticulous personal hygiene, avoiding public places crowded with people, using an electric shaver and limiting the use of scissors and sharp instruments.

6 Teach the patient how to take his own temperature at home. Ensure he has a thermometer and knows what readings are above normal clinical limits.

CORE CARE PLAN   28

Situation Requiring Nursing Intervention

Anaemia

The patient is anaemic due to treatment or the disease process.

Common Potential Problems

Shortness of breath, pallor, tachycardia, palpitations, lethargy and fatigue, difficulty concentrating, increased sensitivity to cold, dizziness and reaction to blood transfusion.

Nursing Intention

1 The signs and symptoms of anaemia will be readily reported by the patient.

2 The patient must be made aware of appropriate self-care measures to minimise anaemia and promote comfort.

3 Any required blood transfusions will be administered safely.

Core Care

1　Provide the patient with information concerning the signs and symptoms of anaemia and emphasise the necessity to report these to medical and nursing staff.

2　Ensure an adequate nutritional intake with a diet rich in protein, vitamins, minerals and iron and that the patient understands the importance of such a diet. Consult the dietitian for specialist advice and support.

3　Monitor the haemaglobin level on a regular basis.

4　Instruct the patient to schedule rest periods and to adjust his activity according to his tolerance level. Assist the patient with any daily activities, as needed, to ensure his safety and conservation of energy.

5　Pay attention to the temperature of the environment and provide extra blankets and clothing if the patient is cold.

6　Observe the patient for any signs of anaemia such as pallor, fatigue and dizziness and report to the medical staff. Ask the patient to rise slowly after sitting or lying and make him aware of other possible safety considerations.

7　Prepare the patient for any blood transfusions, informing him of the purpose and explaining the procedure.

8　Prior to any transfusion check the blood according to the hospital policy to ensure correct identification of the patient and product. Check the prescription and administer any prescribed hydrocortisone and Chlorpheniramine. Administer the blood according to medical orders.

9　Check the vital signs prior to the transfusion and then every 30 min thereafter. Observe for any blood transfusion reaction or circulatory overload. If these occur stop the blood immediately and inform medical staff.

10 Maintain a precise record of intake and output during the transfusion.

Situation Requiring Nursing Intervention

Thrombocytopenia

The patient is thrombocytopenic due to treatment or the disease process.

Common Potential Problems

Minor and major bleeding as evidenced by bruising, petechiae, bleeding gums, nose bleeds, haematuria, conjunctival haemorrhages, headache and blurred vision, change in mental status, haemoptysis and haematemesis and reaction to platelet transfusion.

Nursing Intention

1 The signs and symptoms of minor and serious bleeding will be detected and reported.

2 The patient will be made aware of self-care measures to prevent and minimise bleeding and trauma.

3 Any required platelet transfusions will be administered safely.

Core Care

1   Inform the patient of signs and symptoms associated with minor and serious bleeding and emphasise the necessity to report these to medical and nursing staff.

2   Educate the patient concerning necessary protective measures to help prevent bleeding such as:
   - avoiding the use of a razor, scissors or nail clippers
   - avoiding any forceful nose blowing
   - avoiding straining at defaecation
   - using a soft toothbrush or foam sticks to cleanse the mouth
   - women should avoid using vaginal tampons.

3   Assess the patient regularly for signs of minor bleeding such as:
   - petechiae
   - conjunctival haemorrhages
   - an epistaxis
   - bleeding gums
   - a urinalysis positive to blood
   - bleeding at puncture sites.

4   Assess the patient regularly for signs and symptoms of serious bleeding such as
   - a headache and changes in neurological signs
   - haemoptysis
   - haematemesis
   - haematuria
   - melaena
   - hypotension/tachycardia/orthostatic changes/dizziness. Monitor the pulse and blood pressure regularly. Report any subtle changes to the medical staff.

N.B. The use of a blood pressure cuff may be contraindicated if the platelet count is extremely low, due to the possibility of intense bruising.

5   Avoid any trauma and invasive procedures if possible by:
   • preventing constipation
   • not using rectal thermometers, enemas, suppositories or tampons
   • limiting venepuncture and following this applying firm pressure for 5–10 min
   • refraining from administering drugs by the intramuscular route.

6   Do not administer aspirin or aspirin containing products.

7   Monitor the platelet count daily.

8   Prepare the patient for any platelet transfusion, informing him of the purpose and explaining the procedure.

9   Prior to any transfusion check the platelets according to the hospital policy to ensure correct identification of the patient and product. Check the prescription and administer any prescribed hydrocortisone and Chlorpheniramine. Administer the platelets according to medical orders.

10 Check the vital signs prior to transfusion and then every 30 minutes thereafter. Observe for any platelet transfusion reaction as evidenced by chills, fever, flushing and urticaria. If these occur stop the transfusion and inform the medical staff.

Situation Requiring Nursing Intervention

Neutropenia

The patient is neutropenic due to treatment or the disease process.

Common Potential Problems

Infection of oral mucous membranes, lungs, genitourinary system, perianal area, perineal area, skin and gastrointestinal system (but not always easily detectable) resulting in fever, chills, malaise and patient at risk of developing septic shock.

Nursing Intention

1 Infection will be prevented if at all possible.

2 The onset of infection will be identified early and signs and symptoms reported.

3 Interventions for the treatment of infection will be instituted as early as possible and impending septic shock detected immediately.

Core Care

1 The patient will be provided with information concerning his susceptibility to infection, likely signs and symptoms, necessity to report these immediately and measures he may employ to prevent infection.

2 Institute measures to prevent infections such as:
- ensuring a high calorie, protein and vitamin diet with an oral fluid intake of over 2 l in 24 hours
- protecting the integrity of the skin and mucosa from trauma, invasive procedures and potential sources of infection
- educating the patient on how to perform oral hygiene measures four hourly and in the use of antifungal agents if prescribed
- ensuring the patient employs meticulous body hygiene and that the bed linen is changed daily
- cleansing the room once a day thoroughly and ensuring regularly used equipment is kept for sole use of the patient
- using a consistent and thorough handwashing technique, and wearing a plastic apron when caring for the patient
- minimising patient contact with a lot of people and by the patient nominating a small number of visitors
- educating the patient to choose only cooked food from menu and to avoid raw fruit, salads and vegetables and to drink boiled/bottled water
- instituting protective isolation on consultation with medical and senior nursing staff if deemed appropriate.

3 Measures should be employed to facilitate early detection of infection such as:
- inspecting the body areas with a high potential for infection, i.e. skin, mucous membranes, axillae, perineal and perianal areas
- examining any excretions/secretions for suspicious changes

- recording the vital signs of pulse, blood pressure and temperature four hourly and reporting any subtle changes
- observing for any fever, chills, cough, pain and erythema, reporting to medical staff
- considering if the patient is taking any drugs which would mask the signs of infection such as steroids and antipyretics
- if fever occurs instituting an aggressive search for the site of infection and culturing all potential sites of infection.

4 In the event of infection:
- maintain preventive measures
- control any fever that occurs and employ comfort measures such as tepid sponging, fanning and a cool environment. Administer antipyretics if ordered by medical staff, and evaluate their effectiveness
- ensure adequate hydration to replace fluid lost through sweating
- administer any antibiotics prescribed and in the case of intravenous drugs, using an aspetic technique in all aspects of preparation and administration
- be aware of the impending signs of septic shock such as confusion and irritability, hypotension, fever or hypothermia, oliguria and tachypnoea and report immediately to the medical staff. (See core care plan 38)

Further Reading

The following is a list of articles which give an interesting and informative reference for the nurse involved in providing care for the patient experiencing bone marrow suppression and its attendant problems and challenges.

Brandt, B (1984) A nursing protocol for the client with neutropenia *Oncology Nursing Forum*, **11** (2): 24–28

Brandt, B (1990) Nursing protocol for the patient with neutropenia *Oncology Nursing Forum*, **17** (1), Supplement: 9–15

Carlson, A C (1985) Infection prophylyaxis in the patient with cancer *Oncology Nursing Forum*, **12** (3): 56–63

Collins, C *et al* (1989) Reverse isolation: What patients perceive *Oncology Nursing Forum*, **16** (5): 675–679

Cunningham, R (1990) Infection prophylaxis for the patient with cancer *Oncology Nursing Forum*, **17** (1), Supplement: 16–19

Erickson, J (1990) Blood support for the myelosuppressed patient *Seminars in Oncology Nursing*, **6** (1): 61–66

Gurevich, I and Tafuro, R (1985) Nursing measures for the prevention of

FURTHER READING

infection in the compromised host *Nursing Clinics of North America,* **20** (1): 257–260

Harder, L and Hatfield, A (1982) Patient participation in monitoring myelosuppression from chemotherapy *Oncology Nursing Forum,* **9** (2): 35–37

Henschel, L (1985) Fever patterns in the neutropenic patient *Cancer Nursing,* **8** (6): 301–305

Link, D (1987) Antibiotic therapy in the cancer patient: Focus on third generation cephalosporins *Oncology Nursing Forum,* **14** (5): 35–41

Maxwell, M B (1984) When the cancer patient becomes anaemic *Cancer Nursing,* **7** (4): 321–326

Oniboni A (1990) Infection in the neutropenic patient *Seminars in Oncology Nursing,* **6** (1): 50–60

Rissuccia, M (1985) Haematologic effects of cancer chemotherapy *Nursing Clinics of North America,* **20** (1): 235–239

Rostad, M (1990) Management of myelosuppression in the patient with cancer *Oncolocy Nursing Forum,* **17** (1), Supplement: 4–8

Seminars in Oncology Nursing (1990) Various authors, Blood Component Therapy, **6** (2)

Smeder-Fox, L (1981) Granulocytopenia in the adult cancer patient *Cancer Nursing,* **5** (6): 450–465

Welch, D (1978) Thrombocytopenia in the adult patient with acute leukaemia *Cancer Nursing,* **1** (6): 463–466

Oncology
Emergencies

INTRODUCTION

The patient with cancer is consistently placed at potential risk for the development of serious and often life threatening complications. These complications may be obstructive, metabolic or infiltrative in nature and development may be related to the underlying disease process (as in spinal cord compression) or the treatment (as in tumour lysis syndrome). Such critical situations demand immediate recognition and effective management, although not occurring frequently and sometimes being vague in presentation.

Early recognition and prompt initiation of effective interventions may hopefully promote comfort, enhance a sense of coping and decrease morbidity and mortality. The key attributes of awareness, vigilance and a high level of suspicion are vital if the emergency is to be prevented or detected at an early stage.

The astute nurse should be prepared to provide sophisticated interventions to foster a patient's survival, if, following discussion with the patient, family and caregivers, survival is the desired objective.

The core care plans presented assume the patient is being cared for within a ward environment, but obviously it may be necessary following a thorough assessment of the clinical situation (and in conjunction with the medical staff) to make provisions for the patient to be cared for in the critical care environment.

CORE CARE PLAN   31

Situation Requiring Nursing Intervention

Anaphylaxis

Anaphylaxis resulting from chemotherapy or biotherapy.

Common Potential Problems

Hypotension, tachycardia, arrythmias, compromised breathing (shortness of breath, wheezing and stridor), altered level of consciousness as evidenced by confusion, dizziness and agitations, oedema of the face, eyelids and hands and feet, chest and abdominal pain, nausea and generalised urticaria.

Nursing Intention

1 Prompt identification and appropriate crisis action to minimise the sequelae of anaphylaxis
2 To monitor the patient's condition to detect any deterioration
3 Provision of support to a patient likely to be distressed and fearful

Core Care

Prior to drug administration:

1 Identify the patient at increased risk of anaphylaxis by taking an allergic history. Provide the patient with pertinent information to enable him to identify signs of anaphylaxis and emphasise the need to report these signs immediately if they occur.

2 Prior to any drug administration the nurses should be familiar with the likelihood of the drug causing anaphylaxis, mechanisms of anaphylaxis and have assured access and familiarity with the emergency equipment and likely procedures.

At the first sign of anaphylaxis:

3 Cease the administration of the drug, maintaining intravenous access if already established. Prepare for the possible administration of intravenous hydration.

4 Summon medical and nursing assistance and the emergency equipment.

5 Maintain a patent airway, and if possible a supine position with the feet elevated to an angle of 30–60°, without compromising breathing. Consider the possibility and need for endotracheal intubation and artificial ventilation.

6 Rapidly evaluate subjective and objective symptoms at frequent intervals. Monitor the pulse, blood pressure and respirations (particularly the presence of dyspnoea, altered breath sounds and cyanosis).

7 Prepare to administer adrenaline if necessary.

8 Monitor and evaluate changes in the level of consciousness. If the patient is confused, reorientate in time and place and the reason for being in hospital.

9 Provide psychological support to the patient and his family. Display a calm, competent and confident disposition. Reassure and explain to the patient and any relatives what is being done and what should be expected to happen

shortly. Comfort may be promoted and distress reduced with the administration of analgesics and anti-emetics. Evaluate their effectiveness following administration.

10 Ensure the episode is accurately documented and the patient's sensitivity recorded in appropriate nursing and medical records.

Situation Requiring Nursing Intervention

Carotid Artery Rupture

Common Potential Problems

Severe haemorrhage, obstruction of airway, cardiovascular collapse, cerebral anoxia and fear and anxiety related to awareness of haemorrhage and emergency measures.

Nursing Intention

1 The signs and symptoms of bleeding will be readily reported.

2 The provision of crisis care to maintain the airway, prevent aspiration and restore blood volume if appropriate.

3 Minimisation of fear and anxiety.

Core Care

1 Maintain an awareness of the signs and symptoms indicating impending carotid rupture such as a small amount of bleeding and/or high epigastric/substernal pain. Report to the medical staff immediately if either occur, and make arrangements for the patient to be nursed in a single room if possible and appropriate.

2 In the event of carotid rupture, and it has been determined that the patient shall undergo aggressive emergency measures rather than supportive care:
   • remain with the patient and signal for help
   • minimise blood loss by external constant digital pressure to site of rupture. If the haemorrhage is internal, apply firm pressure to the area behind the tonsillar fossa and with the other hand apply external pressure to the neck
   • maintain an airway by appropriate positioning, ensuring tracheostomy cuff is inflated, or airway is inserted if a tracheostomy is not present. Suction to prevent excess blood leading to aspiration and choking
   • provide oxygen to minimise cerebral hypoxia. The medical staff may wish the patient to attain and remain in a head down position. Monitor for any lowering in level of consciousness, seizures or paralysis
   • ensure in conjunction with the medical staff appropriate venous access is available (a large bore vein or central line). Prepare for the commencement of infusions of intravenous fluid and blood replacement
   • emergency equipment should be made available at the bedside including vascular clamps, oxygen, suction, large absorbable dressings and resuscitation equipment
   • monitor the clinical observations of pulse and blood pressure at frequent intervals. Report any changes to medical staff immediately.

3 Provide psychological support to the patient and his family. Display a calm, competent and confident disposition and reassure and explain to the patient and relatives what is being done and what should be expected to happen shortly. Comfort may be promoted and distress reduced with administration

of analgesic agents as prescribed. Evaluate their effectiveness following administration.

4 Prepare the patient for any proposed emergency surgery. Digital pressure will need to be applied until surgical ligation takes place.

5 When supportive care is to be initiated, rather than resuscitative measures, actions may include the administration of an intravenous opioid such as diamorphine, suctioning to make the patient comfortable and application of large absorbent dressings to soak up the blood. A quiet calm environment where the patient and his family feel supported should be strived for.

6 Ensure other patients and relatives who may experience fear at the sight of a lot of blood are provided time and opportunity to discuss their feelings, and shielded from the main activities.

Situation Requiring Nursing Intervention

Disseminated Intravascular Coagulation

Common Potential Problems

Minor and major bleeding, alteration in fluid balance and decreased oxygen carrying capacity leading to hypovolaemia, hypoxia, hypotension and decreased urine output.

Nursing Intention

1 A prompt identification of the signs of bleeding and progressive disseminated intravascular coagulation.

2 The patient should be made aware of the potential problems.

3 Minimisation of morbidity through diligent monitoring and supportive measures.

Core Care

1 Provide the patient with pertinent information to enable him to identify the signs of early bleeding and emphasise the necessity to report such signs. Educate the patient concerning the use of appropriate self-care measures, expected diagnostic measures and interventions.

2 Protect from environmental injury and avoid:
   - intramuscular and subcutaneous injections
   - rectal temperature readings and suppositories
   - razors
   - vaginal tampons
   - aspirin and other medication interfering with platelet function
   - invasive procedures or traumatic procedures unless absolutely necessary.

Employ:
   - direct pressure to any puncture sites for 5 minutes
   - a soft toothbrush or sponges for oral hygiene.

3 Assess the patient regularly for signs of bleeding or thrombosis of skin, mucous membranes, gastrointestinal tract, genitourinary tract, lungs, central nervous system, retina and the joints.

4 Record the pulse, blood pressure and temperature (sepsis potentiates disseminated intravascular coagulation) four hourly and more often if the clinical condition indicates. Monitor for the signs of blood loss as evidenced by hypovolaemia and altered fluid balance, ie. pallor, dyspnoea, tachycardia, and hypotension.

5 Observe for signs of raised intracranial pressure indicating a possible cerebral bleed such as headache, change in level of consciousness and restlessness.

6 Monitor the urine and stools for signs of blood.

7 Maintain a precise record of intake and output, and report any decrease in urine output to the medical staff.

8 Maintain any infusions of intravenous fluids or blood replacement therapy

as ordered and observe carefully for any transfusion reaction. Stop any blood transfusion immediately if this occurs and inform the medical staff.

9 Administer any heparin as prescribed (this is a controversial treatment).

10 Monitor for signs of hypoxia in the patient and administer any oxygen as prescribed and assess its effectiveness.

11 Monitor the partial thrombin (p.t), partial thromboplastin (p.t.t), fibrinogen levels and clotting factors and report results to medical staff immediately available.

12 Assess for any indications of possible substernal and stabbing chest pain. Administer any prescribed analgesics and monitor their effectiveness. Report the occurrence of any pain to the medical staff.

Situation Requiring Nursing Intervention

Hypercalcaemia

Common Potential Problems

Nausea, vomiting, polyuria leading to thirst and dehydration, constipation, weakness, anorexia, altered level of consciousness as evidenced by confusion, disorientation and psychotic changes, and cardiac arrhythmias.

Nursing Intention

1 The patient should be made aware of the potential problems associated with hypercalcaemia and appropriate self-care measures.

2 Monitoring the patient's condition to enable early detection of a rising serum calcium level.

3 Attain and maintain the calcium level within normal limits (2.1–2.6 mmol/l).

Core Care

1 Provide pertinent information to the patient and family regarding the early signs and symptoms and the necessity to report them, and in addition appropriate self-care measures to maintain a normal calcium level such as increased walking and general physical activity and a fluid intake of over 3 l in 24 hours.

2 Ensure the patient drinks if possible 3 l at least in 24 hours and administer any intravenous hydration as prescribed by medical staff. Assess for the signs and symptoms which indicate fluid overload or dehydration and report to medical staff.

3 Maintain a precise record of intake and output and take a daily weight estimation prior to breakfast during periods of intravenous hydration.

4 Record the pulse and blood pressure four hourly and report any subtle changes to the medical staff.

5 Consider the restriction of dietary calcium following consultation with medical staff and the dietitian.

6 Record any bowel action daily, encourage a high fibre diet and administer aperients if considered necessary.

7 Plan with the patient for periods of rest and activity and emphasise the need to maximise his mobility.

8 Monitor the patient's mental status and be alert for subtle changes which may indicate an impending confusion and possible psychosis. Ask the family to report anything they may notice that indicates a change in the patient's neurological status.

9 If the patient is nauseous and vomiting administer regular antiemetics as prescribed and monitor their effectiveness. Suggest additional measures such as sipping carbonated drinks, eating dry crackers and limiting sudden movements.

10 Administer any pharmacological agents as prescribed to lower calcium level, and monitor the serum calcium level.

Situation Requiring Nursing Intervention

Inappropriate Secretion of Anti-diuretic Hormone

Common Potential Problems

Hyponatraemia causing weight gain, irritability and confusion, weakness and lethargy, anorexia, nausea and vomiting, muscle cramps and seizures.

Nursing Intention

1 The patient should be made aware of the potential problems associated with an inappropriate secretion of anti-diuretic hormone and appropriate self-care measures.

2 Monitoring the patient's condition to enable early detection of a falling sodium level.

3 Attain and maintain a sodium level within normal limits (135–145 mmol/l).

Core Care

1 Provide pertinent information to the patient regarding the early signs and symptoms and emphasise the need to report these along with appropriate self-care measures. The patient may be required to restrict his fluid intake to an amount prescribed by the medical staff and will require advice as to how to achieve this restriction.

2 Maintain a precise record of fluid intake and output and take an estimation of the patient's weight prior to breakfast. Record the specific gravity of all urine collected (norm 1.005–1.025). Monitor the patient for any indications of congestive cardiac failure.

3 Monitor and evaluate recordings of blood pressure, pulse and respirations. Report any subtle changes to the medical staff.

4 Ensure any pain and stress are minimised, as these factors may increase the production of anti-diuretic hormone.

5 Ensure the patient remains free from injury in the event of any seizure. Provide supportive care during and following the event.

6 Monitor the patient for any irritability and confusion and signs indicating a neurological impairment (such as changes in awareness, orientation and behaviour). Report these immediately to the medical staff.

7 Ensure the blood and urine specimens ordered by the medical staff are taken promptly and results given to medical staff when available.

8 Administer any medications as ordered which may include hypertonic intra-venous saline infusions, frusemide and demeclocycline being aware of the expected effects and associated side-effects.

9 If the patient is nauseous and vomiting, administer anti-emetics as prescribed and evaluate their effectiveness. Place a vomit bowl, tissues and mouthwash close to the patient and encourage him to use other additional measures to minimise nausea and vomiting such as sipping carbonated drinks, eating dry

crackers, diversional and relaxation techniques and removal of unpleasant odours, sights and sounds from the environment.

Situation Requiring Nursing Intervention

Intestinal Obstruction

Common Potential Problems

Nausea and vomiting, abdominal distension, pain and cramps, dehydration, hypovolaemia, septic shock and altered nutritional status.

Nursing Intention

1 The early detection of a progressive obstruction and prompt institution of measures to resolve obstruction and associated problems.

2 The provision of comfort measures to minimise symptoms.

Core Care

1 Provide explanations to the patient concerning any proposed procedures, treatments and tests. Ensure the patient is made aware of any preparation necessary for such tests and procedures.

2 Ensure the patient takes nothing by mouth if ordered by the medical staff. Provide appropriate equipment for the performance of adequate oral hygiene and lip lubrication.

3 Administer any intravenous fluids and electrolytes as prescribed. Maintain a precise record of intake and output, take an estimation of the patient's weight prior to breakfast. Ensure the medical staff are aware of any laboratory results, and observe the patient for signs and symptoms of fluid and electrolyte imbalance.

4 Be aware of the possibility of hypovolaemia and septic shock and the early signs and symptoms, report to medical staff immediately if these occur.

5 Record the girth circumference daily in a consistent manner. Provide patient with support to change position to gain comfort.

6 Monitor and report any abdominal pain, noting location, duration and character, administer any analgesics as prescribed and evaluate their effectiveness.

7 Prepare the patient for the possible insertion of a naso-gastric tube. When the tube is in place check the position and patency four hourly, and aspirate and irrigate as ordered. Monitor the volume, colour and odour of any aspirate.

8 Administer anti-emetics to the patient if nauseous and vomiting. Evaluate their effectiveness. Monitor the volume, colour and odour of any vomit, which may be green and bilious, foul tasting and faecal in nature.

9 Administer any drugs prescribed to relieve obstruction such as steroids and monitor the patient for any possible side-effects and a therapeutic effect.

10 Record the pattern of any bowel motions, the amount and consistency, in addition to the presence or absence of flatus. Administer any laxatives, stool softeners or enemas as prescribed, and record their effectiveness.

11 Assess the patient for signs of dehydration such as a decreased urine output, sunken eyes and a dry and warm skin. Report to the medical staff.

12 Prepare the patient for possibility of receiving total parenteral nutrition or surgery.

Situation Requiring Nursing Intervention

Raised Intracranial Pressure

Common Potential Problems

Headache, nausea and vomiting, seizures, altered level of consciousness, motor impairment, sensory deficits, communication difficulties and mood change.

Nursing Intention

1 The signs and symptoms indicating raised intracranial pressure will be readily identified and reported.

2 The patient will be made aware of any expected diagnostic measures and proposed interventions.

3 The physical and psychological sequelae of raised intracranial pressure and its treatment will be minimised and the patient's comfort and safety maximised.

Core Care

1 Educate the patient concerning the potential problems, provide a simple explanation and rationale for procedures, proposed treatments and possible side-effects.

2 Monitor and evaluate changes in status by a neurological examination and report results to the medical staff. Assessment should include examination of any:
   - impaired level of consciousness
   - altered verbal response
   - altered motor response
   - altered pupillary action
   - changed peripheral or mental states. Early signs include irritability, difficulty concentrating and forgetfulness.

3 Monitor and evaluate estimations of the pulse, blood pressure and respirations four hourly. An elevated systolic blood pressure, widening pulse pressure, bradychardia and slowed irregular respirations may indicate a deteriorating condition.

4 Monitor and report the occurrence of a headache (particularly in the morning) and vomiting (which may be projectile). Administer analgesics and anti-emetics as prescribed and evaluate their effectiveness.

5 The location of the tumour will predict the specific clinical manifestations. Provide supportive care and a safe environment following an individual assessment of:
   - communication deficits
   - an alteration in mobility and sensation
   - changes in mood status and cognitive functioning.

6 Monitor the bowel habit and prevent constipation if possible. Straining will cause an increase in intracranial pressure.

7 Ensure the patient remains free from injury in the event of a seizure. Record

the time of onset, part of the body affected first, the duration of the seizure and any change in the level of consciousness.

8   Ensure the emergency resuscitation equipment is close at hand and in working order.

9   Prepare the patient for diagnostic procedures (computerised axial tomography and nuclear magnetic resonance scans) or treatment interventions (radiotherapy and surgical decompression).

10 Administer any steroid therapy, anti-convulsants, hyperosmolar agents as prescribed with an awareness of possible side-effects. Monitor their effectiveness and the anticipated actions of such treatment.

Situation Requiring Nursing Intervention

Septic Shock

Common Potential Problems

Fever, chills, inadequate blood volume, inadequate oxygenation, altered mental status, decreased urine output and disseminated intravascular coagulation.

Nursing Intention

1 Close monitoring of the patient's condition to detect subtle changes quickly which are indicative of progressive septic shock.

2 Institution of active treatment and support measures to reverse septic shock.

Core Care

1   If the patient is neutropenic, maintain any protective and preventive measures as outlined in core care plan 30.

2   Monitor the pulse, temperature, blood pressure and respirations four hourly, more frequent recordings will be required if the patient's condition becomes labile. Report subtle changes (expect a tachycardia, hypotension, hypo- or hyperthermia and tachypnoea as shock progresses) to medical staff.

3   In conjunction with the medical staff, ensure any blood cultures ordered are obtained peripherally and centrally (if a central line is present) along with specimens of urine, sputum, swabs from intravenous infusion sites and cultures of any suspicious lesions. Dispatch to the laboratory promptly.

4   Administer antibiotics immediately prescribed and maintain a strict schedule. Maintain an awareness of and monitor for any side-effects.

5   Maintain a strict record of intake and output. Prepare the patient for the possible insertion of urinary catheter to aid in the precise measurements of urine output. Administer intravenous fluid replacements as ordered and assess their effectiveness as evidenced by an increased tissue perfusion, improved mental status and increased urine output.

6   Assess the skin colour, temperature and moisture. Early shock is evidenced by warm, flushed skin and progressive shock by a cold clammy appearance.

7   Administer humidified oxygen to the patient as ordered instituting oxygen precautions as outlined in the clinical procedure manual. Assess the rate, rhythm, ease of respirations and extent of cyanosis.

8   Administer any antipyretics as prescribed and employ the use of ice packs to axillae, tepid sponging and fanning and maintain a cool environment. Monitor temperature every 30 minutes to assess the effectiveness of these interventions.

9   Monitor the patient's level of consciousness and any restlessness and irritability. Report changes to medical staff immediately.

10 In conjunction with the medical staff ensure specimens ordered for the estimation of acid base balance, urea and electrolytes, full blood count and

blood gases are dispatched promptly. Pass results to the medical staff immediately known.

11 Monitor for possible development of impending disseminated intravascular coagulation (see core care plan 33).

Situation Requiring Nursing Intervention

Spinal Cord Compression

Common Potential Problems

Pain, impaired mobility, sensory loss, alteration in bowel and urinary elimination pattern leading to possible alteration in comfort and potential for injury and disturbance in body image.

Nursing Intention

1 Changes in the patient's neurological status will be readily identified and reported.

2 The patient should be made aware of the signs of progressive spinal cord compression and necessity to report these, expected diagnostic measures and proposed interventions.

3 The physical and psychological sequelae of spinal cord compression and its treatment will be minimised and the patient's comfort maximised.

Core Care

1 Educate the patient concerning the signs of progressive spinal cord compression. Provide simple explanations and rationale for procedures, proposed treatments, limitations in activity and any possible side-effects.

2 Perform a regular neurological assessment of the patient's limb strength, sensation and bowel and bladder function, and report any signs of increasing spinal cord compression as evidenced by:
   - a motor dysfunction – weakness, ataxia, heavy extremities and a paraparesis
   - a sensory loss – numbness, tingling, a feeling of coldness in the affected area and a loss of sensation to pain and temperature
   - constipation and urinary retention.

3 Monitor and record temperature, pulse and blood pressure and maintain an awareness for signs of spinal shock.

4 Assess the location, intensity, duration, radiation and character of pain along with any aggravating or alleviating factors. Administer analgesics as prescribed and monitor their effectiveness.

5 Provide supportive care following individual assessment which may include:
   - early initiation of physical rehabilitation
   - bowel and bladder assistance
   - mobility assistance and measures to minimise sequelae of immobility
   - minimising injury and maintaining correct body alignment.

Liaise closely with the physiotherapist and occupational therapist, and in partnership with the patient, formulate realistic plans for care and support.

6 Prepare the patient for any diagnostic procedures (x-ray, computerised axial tomography, bone scan, myelogram and neurological examinations).

7 Provide support and prepare the patient for any emergency interventions such as a decompressive laminectomy and/or radiotherapy.

8 Administer any steroid therapy as prescribed at meal times to prevent possible damage to the gastrointestinal mucosa, and with antacids if ordered. Monitor for signs indicative of hyperglycaemia, and perform a daily urinalysis for the presence of glucose and acetone. Be aware of the possible development of:

- an increased appetite and weight gain
- the retention of water
- mood changes
- a lowered resistance to infection
- insomnia.

9 Encourage the patient to verbalise his concerns about possible alterations in his role performance, physical dysfunctions and body image. Facilitate the development of a realistic perception of his body image and positive coping mechanisms.

CORE CARE PLAN   40

Situation Requiring Nursing Intervention

Superior Vena Cava Obstruction

Common Potential Problems

Respiratory compromise leading to hypoxia and cerebral anoxia, circulatory compromise leading to facial, arm and trunk swelling, and anxiety and side-effects associated with treatment.

Nursing Intention

1 The provision of supportive care to promote physical and psychological comfort.

2 The early detection of a rapidly deteriorating condition.

3 Minimisation of side-effects associated with proposed treatment.

Core Care

1 Provide the patient with frequent reassurance, with brief and simple explanations of planned procedures and treatments and that an alteration in appearance will resolve with therapy. The patient may be calmed by the presence of a nurse, as he may feel he is suffocating.

2 Monitor the patient for signs of increased respiratory distress and an impending airway obstruction as evidenced by tachypnoea, tachycardia, restlessness, confusion, cyanosis and stridor. Provide a supply of humidified oxygen as prescribed by the medical staff, instituting oxygen precautions outlined in the clinical procedure manual.

3 Position the patient to promote effective use of his respiratory organs and to obtain a maximal respiratory effort. Aid the patient in his performance of necessary activities of daily living with a minimum expenditure of energy.

4 Provide analgesia for any headache and evaluate its effectiveness.

5 Remove any rings and restrictive clothing from the patient. Avoid venepuncture in the patient's arms if possible. Elevate the arms on pillows to enhance venous return and assess the integrity of the skin particularly in oedematous areas.

6 Maintain a precise record of intake and output and perform an estimation of weight prior to breakfast. Administer any diuretics to the patient as ordered, evaluate their effectiveness and observe for any disturbance in fluid and electrolyte balance.

7 Administer steroid therapy to the patient as prescribed at meal times to prevent possible damage to the gastrointestinal mucosa and with antacids if ordered. Monitor for signs indicative of hyperglycaemia and perform daily urinalysis for the presence of glucose and acetone. Be aware of the possible development of:
- an increased appetite or weight loss
- the retention of water
- mood changes
- a lowered resistance to infection

- insomnia.

8 Prepare the patient for any radiotherapy. Monitor the effectiveness of any treatments as evidenced by a decrease in facial and body swelling, a return to normal skin colour, an increased ability to tolerate activity and the resolution of any breathing problems. The patient should experience subjective relief in 72 hours.

Situation Requiring Nursing Intervention

Tracheal Obstruction

Common Potential Problems

Shortness of breath, stridor, tachycardia, tachypnoea, cyanosis, change in level of consciousness, respiratory arrest and fear and anxiety.

Nursing Intention

1 The prompt identification of any obstruction and the use of appropriate interventions to maintain an airway.

2 The provision of support and education to the patient who is likely to be distressed and fearful.

Core Care

1 Educate the patient concerning the signs and symptoms of progressive obstruction and the necessity to report these immediately to medical and nursing staff.

2 Assess the patient for signs and symptoms of progressive obstruction which may include:
   - shortness of breath
   - air hunger
   - stridor
   - use of accessory respiratory muscles
   - pale, cool, moist skin with signs of cyanosis
   - apprehension, restlessness, irritability and a lowered level of consciousness
   - dried secretions around a tracheostomy tube, increasing stomal oedema and progressive difficulty in inserting a tube.

3 Ensure oxygen, suction, humidification equipment and any emergency equipment (including an emergency tracheostomy set) are available and in working order.

4 Administer humidified oxygen to the patient according to medical orders, and institute oxygen precautions as outlined in the clinical procedure manual, evaluate its effectiveness.

5 Maintain an airway with the application of suction if required and monitor the colour, consistency and amount of secretions. Application of humidification may moisten the airway.

6 Monitor vital observations, as the patient's clinical condition indicates, which will include the respiratory rate, rhythm and depth. Report subtle changes to the medical staff.

7 If the patient has a tracheostomy, instruct him in the signs of developing problems such as a mucous plug, dryness, dyspnoea and experiencing difficulty in inserting the tracheostomy tube and appropriate self-care actions.

8 Monitor the patency of the airway by the flow of air upon the hand. If

ineffective airway clearance is apparent in the patient with a tracheostomy, examine any inner tube, possibly reposition the tube and instil normal saline and apply suction. If the problem does not resolve rapidly call the medical staff.

9 Provide a calm environment and make frequent visual and physical contact with patient. The patient is likely to be extremely anxious and distressed and will require supportive reassurance.

10 Provide appropriate equipment to enable the patient to perform adequate oral hygiene to moisten his lips. The patient may require assistance with daily living activities.

11 Be prepared if necessary to assist with an emergency tracheostomy or measures to prepare the patient for emergency surgery or radiotherapy. Warn the patient that obstructive signs and symptoms may worsen initially with radiotherapy.

CORE CARE PLAN   42

Situation Requiring Nursing Intervention
Tumour Lysis Syndrome

Common Potential Problems
Hyperuricaemia, hypocalcaemia, hyperkalaemia, hyperphosphataemia resulting in decreased urine output, impaired renal function, arrythmias, bradycardia, seizures, muscle cramps, weakness, confusion, irritability and numbness and tingling.

Nursing Intention
1 The patient must be made aware of potential complications associated with tumour lysis syndrome and possible self-care measures.
2 Monitor the patient's condition to enable early detection and correction of alterations in electrolytes, with the prevention of renal failure and cardiac arrest.

Core Care
1 Provide pertinent information to the patient at risk regarding signs and symptoms and the necessity to report these promptly, along with appropriate self-care measures. The patient should aim and be encouraged to drink 3 l of fluid a day.
2 Maintain a precise record of fluid intake and output and prepare the patient for the possible insertion of a urinary catheter to aid in the precise measurement of urine output. Administer any intravenous fluid replacements and diuretics as prescribed and be aware of the signs of impending circulatory fluid overload or renal failure.
3 Ensure the patient is weighed at the same hour and evaluate the recording in the light of the presence of oedema and any alterations in blood pressure.
4 Administer allopurinol to the patient as prescribed in order to decrease uric acid formation. Be aware of expected effects and associated side-effects.
5 Administer sodium bicarbonate to the patient as prescribed in order to alkalinise urine. Ensure all urine is examined for clarity, the presence of blood, uric acid crystals and pH. pH should be maintained above the value of 7.0.
6 Monitor and record the vital signs of pulse, blood pressure and respirations. Be alert to subtle changes in the pulse indicating possible arrythmias and report to the medical staff immediately.
7 In conjunction with the medical staff, ensure any blood specimens for the estimation of urea and electrolytes are taken and dispatched immediately. Pass results immediately to the medical staff when obtained.
8 Monitor any change in neurological status – in particular note:
   - sensory alterations – numbness and tingling
   - mood – any irritability and agitation
   - muscle strength – weakness, cramps and twitching
   - level of consciousness – confusion
   - seizures – ensuring the patient remains free from injury. The time of onset, duration and character of the seizure should be recorded and reported to medical staff.

Situation Requiring Nursing Intervention

Hypokalaemia

The patient is hypokalaemic (possibly induced by antibiotics, amphotericin B, diuretic therapy, renal impairment, diarrhoea and vomiting).

Common Potential Problems

Leg cramps, fatigue and weakness, paraesthesia and a compromised cardiovascular system.

Nursing Intention

1 The patient should be made aware of the potential complications associated with hypokalaemia and appropriate self-care measures.

2 Monitoring of the patient's condition to enable early detection of a falling serum potassium level.

3 Attain and maintain the potassium level within normal limits (3.5–5.0 mmol/l).

Core Care

1 Provide pertinent information to the patient regarding the signs and symptoms of a reduced potassium level and emphasise the need to report these symptoms along with appropriate self-care measures to maintain a normal potassium level such as eating bananas, oranges, apricots, legumes, meat and milk.

2 Monitor and report disturbances in the:
  * skeletal muscles – leg cramps, paraesthesia, general weakness and fatigue
  * cardiovascular system – a weakened pulse, decreased blood pressure and tachycardia. Assist the medical staff or a technician to perform an ECG.

3 Assist the patient with activities of living up to his level of tolerance. Encourage him to rest at regular periods.

4 Maintain a precise record of intake and output including gastrointestinal drainage and diarrhoea.

5 Administer any intravenous hydration as prescribed in addition to intravenous potassium supplements. Preferably a concentration of potassium over 80 mmol/l would be infused centrally due to the possibility of peripheral venous spasm and vein sclerosis occurring. If the potassium is infused peripherally observe for any burning, redness, swelling, tenderness and pain. Stop the infusion if these occur and refer to the medical staff. Ensure the potassium is infused at the correct rate.

6 Ensure the patient takes any oral prescribed potassium supplements. Fully dissolve the tablets and ensure the patient drinks the entire solution. Inform the medical staff if the patient is unable to take or tolerate the oral supplements.

FURTHER READING

The following is a list of references from which the nurse may seek information and guidance concerning the care of the patient at risk of being placed in an emergency situation as a result of his disease or treatment.

Arsenault, L (1981) Primary spinal cord tumours: A review and case presentation of a patient with an intramedullary spinal cord neoplasm. *Journal of Neurosurgical Nursing*, **3** (2): 53–58

Baldwin, P D (1983) Epidural spinal cord compression secondary to metastatic disease: A review of the literature *Cancer Nursing*, **6** (6): 441–446

Barry, S (1989) Septic shock: Special needs of patients with cancer *Oncology Nursing Forum*, **16** (1): 31–35

Chernecky, C and Ramsey, P W (1981) *Critical Care of the Client with Cancer* Norwalk: Appleton Century Crofts

Cohen, D (1983) Metabolic complications of induction therapy for leukaemia and lymphoma *Cancer Nursing*, **16** (4): 307–310

Coward, D S (1986) Cancer induced hypercalcaemia *Cancer Nursing*, **9** (3): 125–132

Craig, J and Capizzi, R (1985) The prevention and treatment of immediate hypersensitivity reactions from cancer chemotherapy *Seminars In Oncology Nursing*, **1** (4): 285–291

Cunningham, S (1982) Fluid and electrolyte disturbances associated with cancer and its treatment *Nursing Clinics of North America*, **December**: 579–593

Fruth, R (1980) Anaphylaxis and drug reactions: Guidelines for detection and care *Heart and Lung*, **July/August**: 662–664

Fruth, R (1980) Anaphlylaxis and drug reactions: Guidelines for detection and care *Heart and Lung*, **9**: 622–624

Griffin J and Comley, C (1989) Role of the nurse when the patient with cancer is transferred to the critical care unit *Oncology Nursing Forum*, **16** (5): 705–707

Hartnett, S (1989) Septic shock in the oncology patient *Cancer Nursing*, **12** (4): 191–201

Kane, K K (1983) Carotid artery rupture in advanced head and neck cancer patients *Oncology Nursing Forum*, **10** (1): 14–18

Kreamer, M (1981) Anaphylaxis resulting from chemotherapy *Oncology Nursing Forum*, **8** (4): 13–16

Kirchner, C and Reheis, C (1982) Two serious complications of neoplasm: Sepsis and disseminated intravascular coagulation *Nursing Clinics of North America*, **17** (4): 601–604

Lesage, C (1985) Carotid artery rupture. Prediction, prevention and preparation *Cancer Nursing*, **9** (1): 1–7

FURTHER READING

Lind, J (1985) Ectopic hormonal production: Nursing implications *Seminars In Oncology Nursing*, **1** (4): 251–258

Mahon, S (1989) Signs and symptoms associated with malignancy induced hypercalcaemia *Cancer Nursing*, **12** (3): 153–160

McConnell, E (1983) Septic shock *Nursing Life*, **September-October**: 34–39

Meriney Kryspin, D (1990) Application of Orem's conceptual framework to patients with hypercalcaemia related to breast cancer *Cancer Nursing*, **13** (5): 311–323

Miaskowski, C A (1985) Assessment of acutely ill cancer patients *Seminars In Oncology Nursing*, **1** (4): 230–236

Poe, C and Radford, A (1985) The challenge of hypercalcaemia in cancer *Oncology Nursing Forum*, **12** (6): 29–34

Poe, C and Taylor, L (1989) Syndrome of inappropriate antidiuretic hormone: Assessment and nursing implications *Oncology Nursing Forum*, **16** (3): 373–386

Rooney, A and Haviley, C (1985) Nursing management and disseminated intravascular coagulation *Oncology Nursing Forum*, **12** (1): 15–22

Seminars in Oncology (1978) Oncological Emergencies, Various Authors, 5 (2): 135–140

Seminars in Oncology (1990) Oncological Emergencies, Various Authors, **16** (6): 461–578

Siegrist, C and Jones, J (1985) Disseminated intravascular coagulopathy and nursing implications *Seminars in Oncology Nursing*, **1** (4): 237–243

Sise, J K and Crichlow, R W (1978) Obstruction due to malignant tumours *Seminars in Oncology*, **5** (2): 213–237

Spross, J and Stern, R (1975–1979) Nursing management of oncology patients with superior vena cava obstruction syndrome *Oncology Nursing Society*, **6** (3): 3–5

Yarbro, J (ed) (1981) *Oncologic Emergencies* New York: Grune and Stratton

Cancer Therapies And Their Consequences

INTRODUCTION

The cancer patient may experience a myriad of problems at any one time related both to the disease process and the treatment approach. Alterations in comfort, nutritional concerns and change in elimination pattern all provoke the need for relevant nursing interventions.

Accurate assessment may be facilitated by the fruitful use of an appropriate assessment tool. They are limited in availability particularly in relationship to subjective symptoms such as fatigue and nausea, but a range of tools exist to examine the oral mucosa and nutritional status. A careful assessment will delineate the area of concern for the nurse and patient and provide a basis upon which to direct thought and explore successful strategies of care.

The profile of evaluation has been raised significantly with the exploration of standards of care. Standards once formulated may be fruitfully utilised as a framework for evaluation of patient care. Direct patient evaluation, as to how poorly or how well the specified outcome was achieved is possible in some measurable terms. Standards should be based upon and ideally reflect current nursing knowledge supported by the rapidly expanding body of nursing research.

The range of problems which may arise, as suggested, is extremely broad. All will not be described in the core care plans; attention is focused upon the commonly occurring problems resulting from various treatment strategies.

With commonly occurring situations nurses may fall into routines of response, and forget any alternative or supplementary approaches. The potential role of acupuncture and acupressure, therapeutic massage, relaxation techniques, guided imagery and aromatherapy, to name but a few complementary approaches has not been sufficiently delineated. The use of these approaches should be rapidly examined and exploited following critical research, such as in the control of chemotherapy-induced nausea and vomiting. Their value should not be underestimated particularly in the promotion of a coping response and development of personal strategies to overcome powerlessness in the face of cancer.

CORE CARE PLAN   44

Situation Requiring Nursing Intervention

Insufficient Information Concerning Treatment

Common Potential Problems

The patient has insufficient information concerning treatment and its effects which may be due to a lack of information, selective forgetting, anxious or hopeful distortion, misinterpretation or confusion, and may lead to a lack of participation in decision making, decreased feelings of control, and may discourage effective self-care and potentiate or exacerbate a difficulty in coping.

Nursing Intention

1 To provide complete and accurate information which relates to the patient's situation.

2 Ensure patient understanding and effective maintenance of a level of information given.

3 Ensure the patient is able to act upon such information, encouraging participation in decision making, appropriate self-care and effective coping strategies.

Core Care

1 Prior to the provision of any information establish
   - present levels of information
   - ability to receive new information, eg preferred method of learning and educational ability
   - barriers to effective information giving, eg anxiety, pain, environmental factors
   - degree of information desired and relationship to coping styles.

2 Recognise the individual needs of the patient, and discuss the assessment and suggestions for information giving and the objectives of such sessions.

3 Plan and implement appropriate teaching/information giving sessions with the patient, adhering to basic skills of communication.

4 Monitor the effects of giving information, evaluating knowledge and accuracy, asking the patient to demonstrate or describe key points, giving further input and reinforcement where required. Information giving should be regarded as a dynamic and continuous activity.

5 Where possible and appropriate negotiate inclusion of family or friends to increase the chances of information retention.

6 Ensure information presented is both sequential and logical, the sessions should be brief and if possible relate to what is happening at this particular time, or what will happen shortly.

7 Reinforce any verbal information with other material, for example written booklets, demonstration, posters and video tapes. Consider group teaching as well as one-to-one interaction.

8 Seek help from more skilled and knowledgeable professionals when necessary, and make the patient aware of the community resources information and services available.

Further Reading

Derdiarian, A (1987) Informational needs of recently diagnosed cancer patients. A theoretical framework *Cancer Nursing*, **10** (2) 107–115

Derdiarian, A (1987) Informational needs of recently diagnosed cancer patients. Method and description *Cancer Nursing* **10** (3): 156–163

Dodd, M (1982) Cancer patients' knowledge of chemotherapy – assessment and informational interventions *Oncology Nursing Forum* **9** (3): 39–44

Dodd, M and Ahmed, N (1987) Preference for type of information in cancer patients receiving radiation therapy *Cancer Nursing* **10** (5): 244–251

Fredette, S (1990) A model for improving cancer patient education *Cancer Nursing*, **13** (4): 207–215

Hopkins, M (1986) Information seeking and adaptional outcomes in women receiving chemotherapy for breast cancer *Cancer Nursing* **9** (5): 256–262

Kreamer, K *et al* (1984) Patient education: information about radiation therapy *Oncology Nursing Forum* **11** (4): 67–71

Nichols, K (1984) *Psychological Care and Physical Illness* London: Croom Helm

Webb, P (1990) Patient Teaching In *Excellence in Nursing: the Research Route, Oncology* Faukner, A (ed) Scutari Press: London

Welch–McCafferey D (1985) Evolving patient education needs in cancer *Oncology Nursing Forum* **12** (5): 62–66

Useful booklets are published by

BACUP (British Association For Cancer United Patients)
121/123 Charterhouse Street, London EC1M 6AA

Cancer Link
17 Britannia Street, London WC1X 9JN

Royal Marsden Hospital
Patient Information Series available through:
Haig and Hochland Ltd
International University Booksellers
The Precinct Centre
Manchester M13 3QA

Insufficient information

Situation Requiring Nursing Intervention

Alopecia

Common Potential Problems
Physical discomfort associated with hair loss and damage to scalp. Psychological discomfort associated with distortions in body image and sexuality resulting in feelings of rejection, vulnerability and withdrawal.

Nursing Intention
1 To minimise the psychological impact of hair loss.
2 The patient should be made aware of self-care measures to minimise hair loss, promote comfort and prevent damage to scalp.

Core Care
1 Provide the patient with pertinent information concerning the nature of hair loss, onset, duration and degree of hair loss and the nature of regrowth utilising verbal, written and audio-visual material.
2 Outline measures to minimise hair loss such as:
   • decreasing the handling of remaining hair
   • utilising soft bristle brushes
   • discontinuing the use of hair driers, appliances which produce excessive heat and other possibly harsh hairdressing products
   • using a gentle shampoo.
3 To reduce the patient's discomfort suggest cutting the hair short, shaving any remaining hair and wearing a hair net in bed to prevent hair falling on the pillow.
4 Ensure pillow slips and bed clothes are kept as free from hair as possible.
5 Discuss the availability of a wig and make an appointment with the appliance officer before hair loss occurs so that discussion may take place concerning colour, style and day to day care of a wig.
6 Assure where appropriate, and when the patient meets selection criteria, that measures to prevent alopecia such as scalp cooling are offered.
7 Allow the patient to verbalise feelings concerning hair loss such as anger, resentment and sadness allowing opportunity for exploration of his positive and negative feelings about appearance, reinforce positive perceptions and discuss coping mechanisms. Cutting the hair short may assist in psychological preparation for physical loss, as well as introductions to other patients who have lost their hair.
8 Assist the patient to maintain social contact and promote a personal positive body image. Suggest:
   • wearing own clothes
   • keeping items of meaning and personal interest by the bedside
   • the use of accessories and jewellery
   • make-up to highlight best facial features
   • purchasing a selection of scarves and hats.

9 Outline measures to protect scalp following hair loss such as:
  • the application of high factor sun screen
  • avoidance of extremes of heat and cold
  • protection of scalp with a hat or scarf
  • the application of mineral oil to smooth scalp and reduce itching.

Further Reading

Baxley, K *et al* (1984) Alopecia: Effect on cancer patients' body image *Cancer Nursing*, **7** (6): 499–503

Cline, B (1984) Prevention of chemotherapy induced alopecia: A review of the literature *Cancer Nursing*, **7** (3): 221–228

David, J and Speechley, V (1987) Scalp cooling to prevent alopecia *Nursing Times*, **83** (32): 36–37

Hunt, J (1982) Scalp hypothermia to prevent adriamycin induced hair loss *Cancer Nursing*, **5** (1): 25–31

Lindsey, A (1985) Building the knowledge base for practice, Part 2, alopecia, breast self-exam and other human responses *Oncology Nursing Forum*, **12** (2): 27–34

Parker, R (1987) The effectiveness of scalp hypothermia in preventing cyclophosphamide induced alopecia *Oncology Nursing Forum*, **14** (6): 49–53

Royal Marsden Hospital (1988) *Overcoming Hair Loss. A Guide for Cancer Patients* Booklet No. 16, produced by Patient Education Group Royal Marsden Hospital, London

Tierney, A (1987) Preventing chemotherapy-induced alopecia in cancer patients: Is scalp cooling worthwhile? *Journal of Advanced Nursing*, **12** (3): 303–310

Wager, L and Bye, M (1979) Body image and patients experiencing alopecia as a result of cancer chemotherapy *Cancer Nursing*, **2** (5): 365–369

Situation Requiring Nursing Intervention

Altered Body Image

Alteration in body image resulting from disease or treatment.

Common Potential Problems

An altered body image may result from the diagnosis of cancer, alteration in sexual function and ability to perform sexual activities, depressed libido, fatigue, pain, alopecia, weight change and alterations in appearance, function and concept of a bodily part. These changes may lead to feelings of self-disgust, depression, shame, confusion, guilt, loss of autonomy and sense of control, lack of self-worth, anger, resentment and perhaps hampering expression of femininity and masculinity.

Nursing Intention

1 Determine alterations in the perception of body image and allow the patient freedom of expression concerning feelings associated with this change.

2 Facilitate the building and reinforcement of a healthy perception of body image.

Core Care

1   Prior to any assessment or intervention the nurse should assure herself she has examined her own concerns and resolved issues appertaining to her own body image.

2   Guidance, information and support should be provided to the patient with confidence and skill in a non-judgmental manner in an environment which assures privacy and confidentiality. The nurse should acknowledge her own limitations regarding her counselling skills and the provision of information. Specialist advice should be sought from a clinical nurse specialist, psychosexual counsellor or mental health professional when appropriate.

3   Prior to developing helping strategies the nurse should perform a planned assessment to ascertain feelings about body image and level of knowledge, involving a partner where relevant. Encouragement may be needed to prompt release of feelings, fears, anxieties and concerns.

4   Acknowledge any perceived vulnerability and frustrations as valid and appropriate and recognise possible grief over loss of a former body image.

5   Assist the patient to attain and maintain a desired appearance introducing aids and prostheses as appropriate, and discussing use of clothing and accessories. Praise positive efforts to enhance body image.

6   Encourage verbalisation of positive feelings about the patient by any partner.

7   Adopt an honest, realistic and creative approach to solving problems. Frank informative discussions will provide practical advice and support.

8   Suggest strategies to enhance a sense of accomplishment and foster self-

esteem such as caring for oneself, improving physical appearance, returning to work and social activities and pursuing a physical activity or hobby.

9   Provide information concerning any support and self-help groups applicable to the patient's position and concerns.

10 Acknowledge the value of the individual by enlisting the patient as a team member and co-manager of care with the aim of giving the patient control and decision-making power, diminishing feelings of worthlessness and maximising self-worth and self-control.

Further Reading

Bachers, E (1985) Sexual dysfunction after treatment for genitourinary cancers *Seminars in Oncology Nursing*, **1** (1): 18–24

Blackmore, C (1988) *Body Image: The Oncological Experience*, in Salter, M (ed). *Altered Body Image: The Nurses' Role*. Chapter 10 Chichester: John Wiley

Cooley, M *et al* (1986) Sexual and reproductive issues of the female with Hodgkin's disease (a) An overview of effects. *Cancer Nursing*, **9** (4) 188–193 (b) Application of Plissit Model. *Cancer Nursing*, **9** (5): 248–255

Fisher, S and Levin, D (1983) The sexual knowledge and attitudes of professional nurses caring for oncology patients *Cancer Nursing*, **6** (1): 55–61

Fisher, S (1983) The psychosexual effects of cancer treatment *Oncology Nursing Forum*, **10** (2): 63–68

Lamb, M and Woods, N (1981) Sexuality and the cancer patient *Cancer Nursing* **4** (2): 137–144

Lamb, M (1985) Sexual dysfunction; gynaecologic oncology patient *Seminars in Oncology Nursing*,**1** (1): 9–17

Lion, E ed (1982) *Human Sexuality and Nursing Process* New York: John Wiley

MacElveen-Hoehn P (1985) Sexual assessment and counselling *Seminars in Oncology Nursing*, **1** (1): 69–75

Metcalfe, M and Fischman, J (1985) Factors affecting the sexuality of patients with head and neck cancer *Oncology Nursing Forum*, **12** (2): 21–26

Murray, R (1972) Principles of nursing intervention for the adult patient with body image changes *Nursing Clinics of North America*, **7** (4): 697–707

Price, B (1990) *Body Image – Nursing Concepts and Care* London: Prentice Hall

Shipes, E and Lehir, S (1982) Sexuality and the male cancer patient *Cancer Nursing*, **5** (5): 375–381

Webb, C (1985) *Sexuality, Nursing and Health* Chichester: John Wiley

Situation Requiring Nursing Intervention

Anorexia

Common Potential Problems
Weight loss, increased risk of infection, depression and problems associated with protein/calorie malnutrition.

Nursing Intention
1 The patient will maintain an optimum nutritional status to facilitate health in the presence of disease and treatment.
2 Prevention of further weight loss and attainment and maintenance of a desirable weight.
3 Awareness of potential problems and self-care measures to correct or control altered nutrition.

Core Care
1 Offer explanations concerning the potential consequences of anorexia, contributory causes associated with the disease and treatment and the relationship between health and nutrition.
2 Assess and identify contributory factors such as the disease process, surgery, radiotherapy and chemotherapy and associated problems such as nausea and vomiting, pain, change in mucosa, taste changes and diarrhoea. Anorexia may be induced by pathophysiological mechanisms, treatment or psychological changes, and more commonly a combination of all three.
3 Weigh the patient weekly at the same time of day and record the value ensuring use of the same scale and with the patient wearing similar clothes.
4 Identify with the patient current and previous dietary patterns, appetite variance, preferences and restrictions. Encourage the patient to maintain a food diary. Plan and evaluate appropriate action in the light of assessment.
5 In conjunction with the patient consider manipulation of:
  - intake – gently encourage the patient to eat, with a realistic goal to reach each meal time
    eat a well-balanced diet high in protein and carbohydrates
    eat small and frequent meals and snacks using nutritional supplements
    increase food nutritional value without increasing bulk
    avoid fluid with meals, unless the mouth is dry and sore
    make up 'power-packed' snacks and drinks
    ensure favourite foods and snacks are on hand and encourage to eat whenever hungry
    altering food texture, taste, smell and temperature may be beneficial
    eat slowly and chewing food thoroughly
  - environment – pay attention to the preparation and serving of meals and snacks

employ relaxation and exercise prior to meal times

consider a pre-meal drink of sherry or brandy to stimulate the appetite and promote feeling of well-being

- education – provide printed material on eating difficulties and information on nutrition and food preparation. The patient should demonstrate measures to correct or control altered nutrition.

6 Continually assess effectiveness of the interventions and continue to use those that are successful. Refer to the dietitian if the problem is not managed successfully.

7 Control symptoms that interfere with good nutrition, utilising appropriate pharmacological agents, behavioural management and nursing and self-care interventions.

Further Reading

Butler, J (1980) Nutrition and cancer: A review of the literature *Cancer Nursing*, **3** (2): 13–136

DeWys, W (1979) Anorexia as a general effect of cancer *Cancer*, **43** (5) Supplement: 2013–2019

Donoghue, M, Nunnall, C and Yasko, J (1982) *Nutritional Aspects of Cancer Care* Reston: Reston Publishing Inc.

Holmes, S (1987) Nutritional problems in cancer patients *Nursing*, 3rd Series, **8** (20): 730–738

Holmes, S (1986) Planning nutritional support *Nursing Times*, **82** (16): 26–29

Newell Smith, S (1982) Theories and interventions of nutritional deficit in neoplastic disease *Oncology Nursing Forum*, **9** (2): 43–46

Royal Marsden Hospital (1989) *Overcoming Eating Difficulties. A Guide For Cancer Patients* Booklet No 9, Produced by Patient Education Group Royal Marsden Hospital, London

Schnipper, I (1985) Symptom management – anorexia *Cancer Nursing*, Supplement 1: 33–35

Shaw, C (1989) A taste of things to come *Nursing Times*, **85** (22): 27–28

Tait, N and Aisner, J (1989) Nutritional concerns in cancer patients *Seminars in Oncology Nursing*, **5** (2), Supplement: 58–62

Situation Requiring Nursing Intervention

Bladder Irritability

Irritability resulting from chemotheraphy or radiotherapy.

Common Potential Problems

Haematuria, haemorrhagic cystitis, urinary frequency and urgency, dysuria, suprapubic pain and discomfort and the urge to void.

Nursing Intention

1 The provision of information concerning the cause and appropriate self-care measures.

2 Maximise comfort and maintain a normal pattern of urination.

3 Prevent the development of life-threatening haemorrhagic cystitis.

Core Care

1 Provide the patient with anticipatory instruction concerning the possible occurrence, likely causes and appropriate preventative self-care measures.

2 Ask the patient to report any disruption in normal voiding and any irritative symptoms and change in quantity or appearance of urine. Document any changes in subjective symptoms.

3 Carry out a visual assessment of any urine, in particular the quantity, appearance and presence of blood and odour and record the findings and report changes to the medical officer.

4 Ensure the patient maintains a fluid intake that exceeds 2 l in 24 hours. Anti-emetic therapy should be considered if nausea persists and the possibility of intravenous fluid therapy considered with the medical officer.

5 Administer therapeutic agents ordered, for example, anti-spasmodics, analgesics and sodium bicarbonate. Evaluate their effectiveness. To ensure the urine remains alkaline, encourage the patient to take vegetables in his diet and to drink fruit juice and to avoid irritative substances such as alcohol, tea, coffee and spices.

6 Ensure the toilets are well marked and accessible. If urgency is a problem provide the patient with a selection of appropriate incontinence pads and encourage him to wear easily removable clothing. Liaise with the clinical nurse specialist (continence), if available, and provide psychological support during any periods of embarrassment.

7 Patients receiving bladder toxic drugs such as cyclophosphamide and ifosfamide may:
   • maintain a precise record of intake and output, prior to and for 24 hours following treatment
   • experience retention of urine due to the action of anti-diuretic hormone and require diuretic therapy
   • require catheterisation during high dose chemotherapy

- be instructed to void frequently, and prior to going to bed, thus avoiding the contact of toxic metabolites with the bladder mucosa
- receive substances to protect bladder mucosa, for example, mesna, at prescribed times.

8 If symptoms persist or worsen prepare the patient for any investigations ordered.

9 Be aware of the possibility for the development of life-threatening haemorrhagic cystitis. Be prepared to institute emergency measures and appropriate reassurance and support during periods of fear and anxiety.

Further Reading

Lydon, J (1989) Assessment of renal function in the patient receiving chemotherapy *Cancer Nursing*, **13** (3): 133–143

Goldberg, I *et al* (1984) Urinary tract toxic effects of cancer therapy *Urology*, **132**: 1–6

CORE CARE PLAN   49

Situation Requiring Nursing Intervention

Constipation

Common Potential Problems
Difficult, painful faecal elimination of an irregular and infrequent nature, abdominal distension, cramping, nausea and embarrassment.

Nursing intention
1 Establishment and maintenance of the pattern of elimination in accordance with the patient's usual pattern.
2 Achievement of comfort.
3 Achievement and maintenance of optimal nutritional status.

Core Care
1 Ascertain the patient's normal pattern of elimination and self-care measures used to promote an acceptable bowel habit. Keep an accurate record of bowel activity, noting colour and consistency of stools.
2 Encourage the patient to use self-care measures which have effectively achieved a normal habit in the past.
3 Assess the degree of constipation with a rectal examination if not contra-indicated; consider factors which may place the patient at an increased risk or exacerbate the problem, such as an abdominal or pelvic tumour, dehydration, vinca alkaloid chemotherapy or opiate analgesics, reduced dietary intake and a limited level of activity.
4 Advise the patient about and stress importance of:
   • increasing the amount of fibre foods taken in the diet, seeking advice from the dietitian
   • maintaining a fluid intake of over 3 l in 24 hours
   • promoting physical activity as tolerated
   • maintaining normal patterns and habits of elimination.
5 If the establishment or maintenance of bowel habit is unsuccessful with the above measures, consider the administration oral aperients, suppositories and enemas as prescribed and evaluate their effectiveness over an appropriate time period.
6 Avoid the use of a bed pan if possible and use the bedside commode or toilet to reduce anxiety and embarrassment and increase the amount of privacy possibly helping to maintain the patient's dignity.
7 If the patient is nauseous administer anti-emetics as prescribed and advise about other measures which may be employed to relieve nausea such as sipping carbonated drinks and eating dry crackers. Evaluate their effectiveness.

Further Reading

Cimprich, B (1985) Symptom management: Constipation *Cancer Nursing*, **8**, Supplement 1: 39–43

Harris, W (1980) Bran or aperients *Nursing Times*, **76**: 811–813

Janes, L (1979) Constipation: Keeping a true perspective *Nursing Mirror*, **149** (13), Supplement: i-vi

Regnard, C (1988) Constipation: an algorithm *Palliative Medicine*, **2**: 34–35

Situation Requiring Nursing Intervention

Diarrhoea

Common Potential Problems

Irritation and breakdown of anal tissues, dehydration, electrolyte imbalance, fatigue and weakness, cramping and abdominal pain.

Nursing Intention

1 The establishment and maintenance of patterns of elimination in accordance with the patient's usual pattern.

2 Promote comfort and prevent disruption of skin integrity.

3 Achievement and maintenance of optimal nutritional and hydrational status.

Core Care

1 Ascertain the patient's normal bowel pattern and self-care measures used to promote an acceptable bowel habit.

2 Encourage the patient to use self-care measures which have effectively achieved a normal bowel habit in the past.

3 Assess the degree of severity of any diarrhoea and record the frequency, consistency, volume, presence of blood and colour of stools passed.

4 Review with the patient the potential causes of the problem such as surgery, radiotherapy, drugs, diet, anxiety, infection or faecal impaction. If considering infection as the causative agent, obtain specimens and institute appropriate protective measures.

5 Following each bowel motion wash the perianal area with warm water and mild soap, lubricate the anal area and apply anaesthetic agent to relieve pain as necessary. Apply heat to the abdomen to soothe cramps.

6 Maintain a precise record of intake and output. Make sure the patient takes a fluid intake of 3 l in 24 h and assess him for signs of dehydration and electrolyte imbalance and report to medical staff if present. Monitor electrolyte values, in particular potassium and report abnormal values to medical staff immediately.

7 Encourage the patient to rest when fatigued and to conserve energy in his daily living activities, providing assistance when needed.

8 Administer anti-diarrhoeal, anti-spasmodic and anti-anxiety drugs as prescribed and monitor their effectiveness.

9 Discuss taking a diet with a low residue content and eliminating foods and beverages from the diet likely to irritate the bowel mucosa. Initiate a dietetic referral if this is felt appropriate, and seek advice concerning the osmolarity of any dietary supplements likely to be consumed.

Further Reading

Douglas, A (1975) Diarrhoea *Nursing Times*, **71**: 2022–2023
Jeejeebhoy, K (1977) Definition and mechanisms of diarrhoea *Canadian Medical Association Journal*, **161** (April): 737–739
Regnard, C and Mannix, K (1990) The control of diarrhoea in advanced cancer: A flow diagram *Palliative Medicine*, **4**: 139–142
Smith, D S and Chamarro, T P (1978) Nursing care of patients undergoing chemotherapy and radiotherapy *Cancer Nursing*, **1** (2): 129–134

Situation Requiring Nursing Intervention

Dysphagia

Common Potential Problems

Difficulty swallowing, pain on swallowing, anxiety concerning feelings of choking and aspiration of food and/or fluid leading to a reduced nutritional intake.

Nursing Intention

1 The patient will maintain an optimum nutritional status to facilitate health in the presence of disease and treatment.

2 Appropriate education of the patient concerning the adaptation of the diet to minimise dysphagia and promote comfort.

Core Care

1 Assess in conjunction with a dietitian and speech therapist, the patient's oral cavity, present nutritional status and oral, pharyngeal and oesophageal swallowing. Isolate the cause and present signs and symptoms (which may be due to tumour invasion, surgical resection, infection, stomatitis or dryness as a result of radiotherapy and chemotherapy).

2 Provide the patient with pertinent information concerning the possible cause of the difficulty and appropriate self-care measures to minimise this.

3 Explore the patient's fears and anxieties concerning the possibility of choking and aspiration. Provide education concerning swallowing techniques to minimise aspiration; inhale, place a small amount of food on tongue, swallow, exhale and/or cough and wait 1–2 minutes until next mouthful. Encourage the patient to report the occurrence of choking when swallowing liquids and when food sticks in the throat. Ensure any suction equipment is available and is in working order.

4 Provide suggestions in liaison with dietitian concerning possible modifications to the diet to ease swallowing, and assist with menu choice which may include:
   • small, frequent meals, perhaps 6–8 meals a day, eating little and often
   • modifying the texture and consistency of foods, moistening with sauce and gravies, considering semi-solid and liquid diets
   • taking frequent sips of non-irritating fluid
   • paying attention to position during and following meals, sitting upright and remaining so for 30 minutes following a meal
   • mild flavourings and seasonings may promote palatability
   • considering appetite, food and fluid preferences and type of dysfunction
   • imaginative use of high calorie/high protein fluid supplements.

5 Observe during and after meals for any choking, drooling, regurgitation and foods not tolerated.

6 Consider the use of a speech therapist to improve swallowing ability and the teaching of exercises to improve muscle tone and strength.

7 Assess for the degree and extent of any pain on swallowing. Inspect the oral

cavity for signs of infection or ulceration. Consider the use of systemic and topical analgesics and anti-fungal agents if indicated. Evaluate their effectiveness.

8 If weight loss and symptoms are persistent, consider, in conjunction with the patient, the dietitian and medical staff, the possibility of enteral of perenteral nutrition.

Further Reading

Buckley, J *et al* (1976) Feeding patients with dysphagia *Nursing Forum*, **15** (1): 69–85

Burt, M and Brennan, M (1984) Nutritional support of the patient with oeso-phageal cancer *Seminars In Oncology*, **11** (2): 127–135

McNally, J (1982) Dysphagia *Oncology Nursing Forum*, **9** (1) 58–60

Regnard, C. (1990) Managing dysphagia in advanced cancer – A flow diagram *Palliative Medicine* **4**: 215–218

Situation Requiring Nursing Intervention

Dyspnoea

Common Potential Problems

Uncomfortable and unpleasant breathing patterns leading to hypoxia, alteration in ability to perform daily living activities, fatigue, fear and anxiety and an altered mental status.

Nursing Intention

1 Establishment and maintenance of effective breathing patterns with the maximum conservation of energy.

2 The patient will be made aware of self-care measures and nursing interventions to maintain adequate respiratory function.

Core Care

1 Regularly observe the patient's rate, rhythm and depth of respirations, pulse, temperature, chest wall movements, ease of breathing and mental status. Report any subtle changes to medical staff.

2 Describe and record abnormalities in sputum production, such as its tenacity and signs of infection. Identify any contributory causes of dysponea, eg infection, anxiety, pulmonary embolus, superior vena cava obstruction, primary or secondary lung involvement, pericardial effusion, pleural effusion and radiotherapy or chemotherapy induced damage to the lung.

3 Inform the patient of plans for and purpose of any diagnostic or treatment measures such as a chest x-ray, full blood count, arterial blood gases, pleural aspiration and radiotherapy.

4 Institute measures to help reduce unpleasant and uncomfortable breathing and to promote effective physical and psychological coping mechanisms such as:

- breathing techniques – assist and instruct the patient in techniques which will increase tolerance to dyspnoea which includes slow deep breaths, and exhalation longer than inhalation. Liaise with the physiotherapist for help and advice

- positioning – allow the patient to adopt a suitable position to reduce breathlessness. Sitting up and slightly leaning forward is normally beneficial, which promotes maximum relaxation of the chest and freedom of movement of the lower chest. Sit on the edge of the bed with arms folded and leaning on a bedside table or sitting in the chair, with feet wide apart, elbows resting on knees may help

- emotional support – the presence of a nurse is reassuring and particularly one who is close by and quickly available. Provide a calm environment and offer gentle and sure explanations

- relaxation techniques including massage, music and aromatherapy

- increase air movement over the patient's face by opening a window or use of a fan

- planning for activity – maximise the potential for activity, carrying out daily living activities as tolerated. Refer the patient to the occupational therapist if appropriate and plan his activity around frequent rest periods
- oxygen therapy – administer humidified oxygen as prescribed by medical staff and assess its effectiveness. Employ precautions as outlined in the clinical procedure manual, and offer adequate oral care to maintain a moistened oral mucosa
- pharmacological agents – administer any sedatives, diuretics, antibiotics, narcotics, steroids or bronchodilators as prescribed, and assess their effectiveness and maintain an awareness for potential side-effects.

Further Reading

Brown S and Mann, R (1990) Breaking the cycle, control of breathlessness in chronic lung disease *Professional Nurse*, **4** (6): 325–328

Foote, M *et al* (1986) Dyspnoea: A distressing sensation in lung cancer *Oncology Nursing Forum*, **13** (5): 25–31

Regnard, C and Almedzai, S (1990) Dyspnoea in advanced cancer – a flow diagram *Palliative Medicine*, **4**, 311–315

Rokosky, J (1981) Assessment of the individual with altered respiratory status *Nursing Clinics of North America*, **16** (2): 195–206

Wickham, R (1986) Pulmonary toxicity secondary to cancer treatment *Oncology Nursing Forum*, **13** (5): 69–76

Zehner, L and Hoogstraten, B (1985) Malignant pleural effusions and their management *Seminars In Oncology Nursing*, **1** (4) 259–268

Situation Requiring Nursing Intervention

Extravasation

Suspected extravasation of a vesicant cytotoxic drug given by the intravenous route. (Common vesicants include vincristine, doxorubicin, actinomycin D and mitomycin C).

Common Potential Problems

Immediate pain, burning sensation, erythema, swelling over 1–4 weeks leading to discolouration of the skin, fibrosis of blood vessels, induration, blistering erosion of tissue resulting in ulceration, necrosis and infection and possible functional impairment.

Nursing Intention

1 Rapid detection of a suspected extravasation

2 Through appropriate action, minimising physical damage and pain (maintaining skin and vessel integrity)

3 Minimising patient anxiety and providing information to facilitate appropriate self-care actions.

Core Care

1 Prior to administration, explain to the patient the importance of alerting the nurse to any sensation of burning or stinging or any other acute change around the area of the needle or cannula.

2 Extravasation should be suspected when:
   - the patient complains of a sharp burning/stinging sensation around the needle or cannula
   - swelling or leakage occurs at the site of the needle or cannula
   - resistance is felt on the plunger of the syringe during bolus administration
   - lack of blood return into the syringe occurs, but if found in isolation this should not be regarded as an indication of a non-patent vein
   - the flow of fluid is absent or slowed during an infusion.

   A natural redness may occur during the administration of doxorubicin along the vein, and many drugs are extremely cold on removal from refrigeration and the feeling of cold should be distinguished from a burning sensation.

3 The treatment of a suspected extravasation is controversial and varies from centre to centre, *consultation* with the local nursing policy, procedure, pharmacists and medical staff is recommended. A frequently recommended procedure encompassing immediate action and subsequent management for suspected or confirmed extravasation is detailed below:
   - stop administration immediately
   - if possible withdraw any solution and blood by pulling back on a syringe and then remove the needle or cannula
   - cover area with an ice pack and elevate the extremity (heat packs may be recommended in the extravasation of vincristine)
   - inform the medical officer and on prescription prepare hydrocortisone

100mg/2ml or dexamethasone 8mg/2ml for injection (or other antidotes, eg. hyaluronidase for vincristine), inject 0.1–0.2ml subcutaneously at the points of a compass around the circumference of the area of extravasation, using a new needle for each injection, ensuring the whole area is infiltrated
- re-apply ice packs to the area for 24 hours, again elevating the extremity and encouraging a full range of motion
- apply hydrocortisone cream 1% on prescription twice daily covering with a non-adherent occlusive dressing, this is continued as long as erythema persists. Instruct the patient how this may be done.

4 Document the incident according to local policy, information will normally include:
- patient details, time, date and location
- insertion site, needle type, amount and concentration of drugs, sequence of drug administration and technique used (bolus or infusion)
- nursing and medical action taken
- patient complaints, comments and statements.

5 All actions taken should be explained honestly to the patient, seeking consent and co-operation. Ensure any anxieties and concerns are explored, providing written explanations to reinforce verbal conversations if necessary.

6 Observe the site regularly for indications of erythema, induration, blistering or necrosis. Patients should be asked to observe the site daily and report any increasing discomfort, peeling or blistering of the skin immediately.

7 Encourage the patient to verbalise any sensation of pain or increased discomfort and provide analgesia accordingly, evaluating the effectiveness at appropriate intervals.

Further Reading

Inoffo, R and Friedman, M (1980) Therapy of local toxicities caused by extravasation of cancer chemotherapeutic drugs *Cancer Treatment Reviews*, **7**: 17–27

Larson, D (1985) What is the appropriate management of tissue extravasation by anti-tumour agents? *Plastic Reconstructive Surgery*, **75** (3): 397–402

Montrose, P (1987) Extravasation management *Seminars In Oncology Nursing*, **3** (2): 128–132

Smith, R (1985) Extravasation of intravenous fluids *British Journal of Parenteral Therapy*, **6** (2) 30–42

Smith, R (1985) Prevention and treatment of extravasation *British Journal of Parenteral Therapy* **6** 5: 114–120

Stuart, M (1982) Sequence of administering vesicant cytotoxic drugs *Oncology Nursing Forum*, **9** (1): 53–54

CORE CARE PLAN 54

Situation Requiring Nursing Intervention

Fatigue

Common Potential Problems
Perceptions of continual tiredness, lack of energy, unable to carry out expected daily activities, depression and impaired nutrition and comfort.

Nursing Intention
1 Identification of all possible factors contributing to fatigue.
2 Alleviation and minimisation of the identified causes of fatigue.
3 Establishment and maintenance of maximal independent activity, comfort and nutrition.

Core Care
1 Assess and identify with the patient clues to the possible causes of fatigue which may be normal, pathophysiological, situational or psychological in nature, or a combination of all these factors. Manifestations of fatigue include alterations in general appearance, subjective descriptions, attitude, speech, activity and concentration.
2 Identify patterns of fatigue such as: when greatest, the length of time it persists, the intensity, aggravating and alleviating factors, impact upon life-style, usual patterns of sleep and rest, any immobility, sensory deprivation and depression.
3 Provide information and support to the patient to enable him to prevent or manage levels of depleted energy, in conjunction with the occupational therapist if appropriate, such as:
   - rest when fatigue is experienced, especially prior to and following therapy
   - fatigue is a temporary effect
   - maintain life patterns if possible, with a pace consistent with varying energy levels
   - plan for consistent periods of exercise and rest
   - seek assistance and resources when unable to perform daily activities or when required to expend a large amount of energy.
4 In conjunction with the patient:
   - set priorities for use of available energy
   - schedule activities and procedures so rest periods are planned
   - ensure pain is controlled and the patient adequately nourished and other symptoms aggravating fatigue are minimised.
5 Consult with the medical staff concerning treatment of any underlying anxiety and depression. Consider referral to a psychological support service. Explore any existing emotional stressors with the patient and provide emotional support and encourage effective coping behaviours.

Further Reading

Aistars, J (1987) Fatigue in cancer patients: a conceptual approach to a clinical problem *Oncology Nursing Forum*, **14** (6): 25–30

Kobashi-Schoot, J *et al* (1985) Assessment of malaise in cancer treated with radiotherapy *Cancer Nursing*, **8** (6): 306–313

Piper, B *et al* (1987) Fatigue mechanisms in cancer patients: Developing a nursing theory *Oncology Nursing Forum*, **14** (6): 17–23

Ryden, M (1977) Energy: A clinical consideration in the nursing process *Nursing Forum*, **16**: 71–82

Varrichio, C (1985) Selecting a tool for measuring fatigue *Oncology Nursing Forum*, **12** (4): 122–127

Wood, C (1990) Measuring vitality *Nursing Times*, **86** (19): 26–28

Rhodes, V *et al* (1988) Patients' descriptions of the influence of weakness and tiredness on self-care abilities *Cancer Nursing*, **11** (3): 186–194

CORE CARE PLAN   55

Fever, Rigors and Sweats

Common Potential Problems
Rigors, sweating, alteration in comfort, malaise, dehydration and anorexia.

Nursing Intention
1 Identification of the cause of the fever with prompt treatment to help restore the body temperature to normal.
2 Provision of an acceptable level of comfort.
3 Prevention of problems and complications associated with an unremitting fever.

Core Care
1 Monitor and record the patient's temperature four hourly and more often if clinical condition indicates. Ensure the temperature is taken at same site to promote consistent results.
2 Assess for any possible signs of sepsis or hypothermia, recording pulse and blood pressure four hourly. Report subtle changes to the medical staff.
3 Instigate a search for the possible cause of the fever. Possible sites of infection may include the lungs, mouth, urinary tract and intravenous and drain site insertions.
4 Stop any transfusion or therapy suspected of causing fever and rigors. Report to the medical staff. Administer any medications such as hydrocortisone and chlorampheniramine and evaluate their effectiveness.
5 Provide blankets during a rigor, remove them during sweats. Reassure the patient that the rigor will pass, and remain with him during the event.
6 Employ body cooling techniques such as fanning, tepid sponging and administration of prescribed anti-pyretics, and evaluate their effectiveness. Remove and replace any wet bedding and clothing when damp, and position the patient in a well-ventilated environment.
7 Minimise the metabolic demands and fatigue by assisting the patient with daily activities. Encourage periods of rest.
8 Maintain a precise record of intake and output, rehydrating with oral and intravenous fluids as ordered, and assessing for signs of dehydration.
9 Provide appropriate nutritional support if the patient is anorexic.

Further Reading

Cunha, B, Beltran, M and Gobbo, P (1984) Implications of fever in the critical care setting *Heart and Lung*, **13** (5): 460–465
Davis-Sharts, J (1978) Mechanisms and manifestations of fever *American Journal of Nursing*, **78**: 1874–1876

Henschel, L (1985) Fever patterns in the neutropenic patient *Cancer Nursing*, 8 (6): 301–305

Mandell, L (1983) Management of the febrile neutropenic patient *Journal of the Canadian Medical Association*, April: 915–918

Situation Requiring Nursing Intervention

Infertility

Potential alteration in fertility resulting from chemotherapy or radiotherapy.

Common Potential Problems

Lack of knowledge and appreciation of alterations in fertility (for example: oligospermia, azoospermia, amenorrhoea and irregular menses and potential mutagenic and teratogenic effects), importance of not becoming pregnant and appropriate and safe methods of contraception, and anger, resentment and grief at the loss or potential loss of reproductive function.

Nursing Intention

1 Provision of appropriate guidance and education concerning alterations in fertility and selection of methods of contraception.

2 Initiating support for the patient and any significant other to facilitate realistic coping with any alteration in fertility.

Core Care

1 Assure a safe atmosphere and an environment of privacy and confidentiality for the patient whilst discussing any issues likely to evoke embarrassment.

2 Appropriate guidance and education may only follow assessment of individual circumstances. Assessment points may include identification of the potential effects of cancer therapy on gonadal functioning and the patient's and partner's knowledge, a brief sexual history concerning reproductive and contraceptive issues, current fertility status and desires for future child bearing.

3 Provision of information, verbal and written, will be dependent upon the individual's treatment, age, gender and desire for a future family
It may include:
  • the potential effects of cancer therapy on fertility and an undetected pregnancy, and in women, the potential effect of treatment on menstruation
  • potential duration of infertility if temporary
  • exploration and advice concerning alternatives for reproduction, for example sperm banking, artificial insemination and adoption
  • discussion of the rationale for and methods of contraception available during and following treatment. Contraceptive hormones may be contraindicated. Barrier and natural methods of contraception should be discussed. Natural methods are not advised during or within two years of treatment. Assist the patient to make a decision concerning contraception in the light of knowledge and past experience.

4 Initiate discussion and a time for reflection with the patient and partner concerning feelings and attitudes to alterations in fertility. Promote the ventilation of feelings regarding loss or threatened loss of reproductive function and realistic expectations concerning the return of function.

5 Allow opportunity for the patient to redefine their own sexuality without the

possibility of procreation, facilitating the development of self-worth independent of the activity of parenting.
6 Seek specialist advice and information when appropriate from a person with
specialist knowledge concerning effects of cancer treatment on reproduction,
appropriate management and counselling skills.

Further Reading

Frank-Stromborg, M (1985) Sexuality and the elderly cancer patient *Seminars
In Oncology Nursing*, **1** (1): 49–55
Kaempfer, S (1981) The effects of cancer chemotherapy on reproduction: A
review of the literature *Oncology Nursing Forum*, **8** (1): 11–18
Kaempfer, S *et al* (1983) Sperm banking, a reproductive option in cancer
therapy *Cancer Nursing*, **6** (1): pp 31–38
Kaempfer, S (1985) Fertility considerations and procreative alternatives in
cancer care *Seminars In Oncology Nursing*, **1** (1): 25–34
Krebs, L (1985) Pregnancy and cancer *Seminars In Oncology Nursing*, **1** (1):
35–41
MacElveen–Heohen, P (1985) Sexual assessment and counselling *Seminars In
Oncology Nursing*, **1** (1): 69–75
Peters, R (1981) Overview of contraception *Oncology Nursing Forum*, **8** (1):
38–39
Tarpy, C (1985) Birth control considerations during chemotherapy *Oncology
Nursing Forum*, **12** (2): 75–78
Yarbro, C and Perry, M (1985) The effect of cancer therapy on gonadal function
Seminars In Oncology Nursing, **1** (1): 3–8

Situation Requiring Nursing Intervention

Infusion of Amphotericin B

Common Potential Problems
Fever, severe chills, joint and muscle pain, hypokalaemia, nephrotoxicity, phlebitis, anaphylaxis and anaemia (in the long term).

Nursing Intention
1 Amphotericin B therapy shall be given safely, and the signs and symptoms of a reaction will be readily identified and treated.

2 The patient will be made aware of the nature of the therapy and potential problems and actions to avert such problems.

Core Care
1 An explanation should be made available to the patient concerning the nature and necessity for this therapy, associated side-effects and potential toxicities and measures to be taken to minimise these.

2 Administer the amphotericin B infusion according to hospital protocol, each day or every other day, and following appropriate reconstitution in 5% dextrose with a pH above 4.2. Protect from the light and employ the aid of an infusion device to ensure correct rate of delivery over specified period of time, usually 6 h.

3 If possible on consultation with the medical staff avoid infusion of the drug into a peripheral vein and employ the use of central line to prevent the occurrence of phlebitis.

4 Prior to maintenance therapy being instituted, a test dose and escalation of dose are carried out to assess the patient's sensitivity to the drug. Monitor the patient at half hourly intervals during this time, and in particular for signs of impending anaphylactic shock. Record the blood pressure, pulse and temperature and report subtle changes to the medical staff.

5 Administer a pre-medication of intravenous hydrocortisone and chlorphenira-mine 30 minutes prior to infusion, and possibly 2 hours into the infusion and at regular intervals thereafter, in accordance with the prescription. Observe the patient for any infusion reaction and in such an event:
   - cover the patient with warm blankets during rigor
   - administer additional medication to control a rigor and lower the patient's temperature if the time since the last administration of such drugs allows. Evaluate their effectiveness. If the reaction does not subside, stop the infusion and call the medical staff
   - reassure the patient that the reactions will pass quickly
   - emergency drugs and resuscitation equipment should be close at hand and in working order. Be alert for the signs of impending anaphylaxis as evidenced by a decreased pulse, urticaria, cyanosis and shortness of breath (see core care plan 31)

- Monitor clinical signs regularly and report subtle changes to the medical staff immediately.

6 In conjunction with the medical staff, monitor serum potassium values prior to each infusion and on a daily basis. Assess the patient for signs of hypokalaemia which may include lethargy, muscle cramping and dysrhythmias. Administer oral or intravenous potassium supplements in the appropriate manner if prescribed.

7 Record the patient's intake and output precisely and monitor for signs of any nephrotoxicity. Evaluate renal function tests daily and inform the medical staff of any abnormal results immediately, it may necessitate a dosage alteration.

8 In conjunction with the medical staff, monitor the haemoglobin value and observe for signs of anaemia on a regular basis and maintain an awareness that this problem may appear up to 6–8 weeks following commencement of therapy.

Further Reading

Anderson, B and Faulkner, W (1982) Amphotericin B: Effective management of adverse reactions *Cancer Nursing*, 5 (6): 461–464

Corner, J (1981) Amphotericin B: Ten common questions *American Journal of Nursing*, **81** (6): 1166–1167

Holtzclaw, B (1990) Control of febrile shivering during amphotericin B therapy *Oncology Nursing Forum*, **17** (4): 521–528

Holtzclaw, B and Rutledge, B (1990) Use of amphotericin B in immunosuppressed patients with cancer. Part two: Pharmocodynamics and nursing implications *Oncology Nursing Forum*, **17** (5): 737–744

Parker, R H (1981) The role of amphotericin in life threatening fungal infections *Drug Therapy* Oct: 71–74

Rutledge, D and Holtzclaw, B (1990) Use of amphotericin B in immunosuppressed patients with cancer. Part One: Pharmacology and toxicities *Ontology Nursing Forum*, **17** (5): 731–736

CORE CARE PLAN   58

Situation Requiring Nursing Intervention

Insomnia

Common Potential Problems
Restlessness, irritability, fatigue, lethargy and a decreased level of alertness.

Nursing Intention
1 Promoting the absence of an unacceptable sleep disturbance.
2 The patient should be made aware of the self-care and nursing interventions to promote a restful and uninterrupted sleep.

Core Care
1   Obtain information from the patient concerning his sleeping habits, the usual amount of sleep and measures taken to promote sleep at home. Consider the presence of a sleep disturbance, and whether it is a difficulty falling asleep, inability to remain asleep or early morning awakenings.

2   Pay attention to the patient's sleep environment and ensure it resembles his usual sleep environment as closely as possible. Ensure any bedding, the patient's position, level of ventilation, temperature of the room and noise level are satisfactory.

3   Adhere to the patient's usual sleep/wakefulness routine in addition to usual bedtime and napping habits.

4   During the day maintain a level of activity comparable with the patient's energy levels, avoiding prolonged time in bed when not sleeping and encouraging daily physical exercise not less than 2 hours prior to bedtime. Relaxation during the day may help to induce sleep at night, and consider the use of aromatherapy and massage.

5   Allow the patient opportunity for discussion of any anxieties, encouraging the sharing of current concerns and fears. Consider the prescription of antidepressant or anxiolytic drugs in conjunction with the medical staff.

6   Be aware of factors which may promote an interruption in the patient's sleep, such as disturbing and frightening dreams, sleeping in a shared area, the uncomfortable weight of heavy bedclothes, pain, night sweats, a cough, episodes of dyspnoea and urinary frequency, taking appropriate action to relieve or minimise such problems. Review all the patient's medication and its possible detrimental effect on sleep.

7   Ensure the patient isn't hungry prior to sleeping, but avoid heavy meals. A high protein snack (L-tryptophan being a precursor of serotonin, and serotonin promotes the onset of sleep) and beverages devoid of caffeine may induce sleep.

8   Maximise the patient's comfort and consider the use of diversional strategies such as television, music, reading, conversation and massage.

9   If there is no response to non-pharmacological and symptom control measures, employ the judicious use of sleep inducing drugs on a short term basis

according to hospital prescription and evaluate their effectiveness. Explain the possible effects and side-effects to the patient.

10 Avoid awakening the patient during the night, and co-ordinate care activities to coincide with spontaneous awakening or a single awakening if possible. Consider the scheduling of tests, investigations and medications.

Further Reading

Beszterczey, A and Lipowski, Z J (1977) Insomnia in cancer patients *Canadian Medical Association Journal*, **116**: 355

Cannice, J P (1980) Treatment of insomnia in cancer patients using muscle relaxation training *Disseration Abstracts International*, (b), **40** (12): 5803

Hauri, P *et al* (1985) Sleep in cancer patients *Sleep Research*, (Abstract), **14**: 237

Lamb, M A (1982) The sleeping patterns of patients with malignant and non malignant disease *cancer nursing*, **5** (5): 389–396

Situation Requiring Nursing Intervention

Nausea and Vomiting

Common Potential Problems

Fluid and electrolyte imbalance, discomfort, weakness and fatigue and altered nutritional requirements.

Nursing Intention

1 Identification of potential and actual causes of nausea and vomiting.

2 Interventions to maintain comfort, nutrition and hydration.

3 Elimination of the nausea and vomiting if at all possible.

Core Care

1 Identify the interventions used by the patient in the past to relieve nausea and vomiting, encourage him to use these and suggest appropriate additional self-care measures.

2 Record the pattern, onset, frequency, duration and intensity of symptoms and any aggravating and alleviating factors, considering the various aetiological mechanisms which may be in operation.

3 Record intake and output precisely noting the volume and character of any vomit. Evaluate the patient for hydrational and electrolyte imbalances and inform the medical staff immediately.

4 Minimise the sights, sounds, smells that may initiate nausea, and promote rest in a comfortable environment limiting sudden rapid movements.

5 Provide a bowl and tissues in close proximity to the patient and remove vomit immediately from bedside. Ensure facilities for the maintenance of oral hygiene are available, and provide supportive reassurance during periods of vomiting.

6 Suggest and explore the use of distraction, relaxation with music, guided imagery, and acupressure with the patient as a means of controlling nausea and vomiting.

7 Assess the patient's food preferences and tolerances, cold foods without spices and bland in nature are usually better tolerated. Carbonated drinks sipped slowly may relieve nausea, as well as eating dry toast and crackers.

8 Administer appropriate anti-emetics as prescribed on a regular basis appropriate to the pattern of nausea and vomiting. Evaluate their effectiveness and if symptoms persist report to the medical staff and consider changes in dosage, administration schedule and type of antiemetic employed.

Further Reading

Contanch, P (1983) Relaxation training as an antiemetic intervention *Cancer Nursing,* **6** (4): 277–283

Frytak, S and Moertel, C (1981) Management of nausea and vomiting in cancer patients *Journal of the American Medical Association*, **245**: 393–396

Laszlo J (ed) (1983) *Anti-Emetics and Cancer Chemotherapy* London: Williams and Wilkins

Lindsey, A (1985) Building the knowledge base for practice, Part 2, nausea and vomiting *Oncology Nursing Forum*, **12** (1): 49–56

Rhodes, V *et al* (1987) Patterns of nausea, vomiting and distress in patientsreceiving anti neoplastic drug protocols *Oncology Nursing Forum*, **14** (4): 35–43

Stannard, D (1989) Pressure prevents nausea *Nursing Times*, **85** (4): 33–34

Warren, K (1988) Will I be sick nurse? *Nursing Times*, **84** (11): 30–31 *Nursing Times*, **84** (12): 30–31

Yasko, J (1985) Holistic management of nausea and vomiting caused by chemotherapy *Topics in Clinical Nursing*, **7** (April): 26–36

Situation Requiring Nursing Intervention

Altered Skin Integrity

Alteration in skin integrity associated with radiotherapy.

Common Potential Problems

Erythema, dryness, pruritus, flaking, ulceration with weeping, pain and discomfort and alteration in body image.

Nursing Intention

1 The patient should be made aware of potential skin changes and appropriate self-care measures to maintain and restore skin integrity.

2 The patient will experience minimal physical and psychological discomfort associated with any skin changes.

Core Care

1 Provide the patient with pertinent verbal, written and audio-visual information concerning the effects of radiation on the skin, the possible onset, duration and nature of effects and appropriate self-care measures to maintain the integrity of skin. Emphasise to the patient the necessity of reporting changes to the health care team.

2 Remain vigilant and inspect the status of the skin on a daily basis (this should include the area exposed to radiation and the site of the exit beam) and note in particular the colour, moisture, any scaling and temperature of the skin. Ask the patient about the degree of tenderness and presence of any itching. If drainage is present from the skin, note the colour, odour, amount and consistency of any exudate.

3 Ensure the patient is aware of the following points to help prevent trauma and irritation to the appropriate site:

- wearing non-constrictive clothing around the site of radiation, for example soft collars, avoiding bra straps and belts and encouraging clothing which is 100% cotton in nature
- avoiding rubbing, unnecessary friction (encourage to refrain from scratching) exposure to wind and extremes of hot and cold (avoiding ice packs and hot water bottles), harsh laundry products, perfume, underarm deodorants, after shave, commercial skin products and creams. Encourage men to shave with an electric shaver, cuts infected will be slow to heal
- a light dusting of baby powder may soothe itching
- avoiding direct sunlight by wearing a hat or light clothing. Ensure the patient uses a sunscreen of factor 15 when radiotherapy is completed
- in consultation with the radiotherapist and therapeutic radiographer, warm water and mild soap may be used to cleanse the patient's skin, pat the area dry, avoiding rubbing and vigorous wiping actions. Advise the patient to take care not to wash away any ink markings. Particular care should be taken of the skin found at the folds, for example under breasts, between buttocks, the groin and behind ears, if the area is being irradiated.

4 Consider the patient's nutritional status, a high protein, balanced diet will help to maintain skin integrity and promote healing. Consult with the dietitian if necessary.

5 In the event of dry desquamation occurring, consider the application of creams or lotions such as lanolin or hydrocortisone to the affected area, in conjunction with the radiotherapist. Ensure only a thin layer of cream or lotion is applied and the area cleansed between applications.

6 In the event of moist desquamation occurring and in liaison with the radiotherapist, irrigate the area with warm water or saline, dry the area carefully and apply an appropriate protective non-adherent dressing, avoiding placing the tape within the radiation field. Maintain vigilance for a further deterioration, pain and signs of infection.

7 Provide opportunity for the patient to explore his feelings and possible resentment and anxiety concerning long-term and short-term skin changes induced by radiation.

Further Reading

Bloomer, W and Hellman, S (1979) Normal tissues responses to radiation therapy *New England Journal of Medicine*, **293**: 80–83

Oncology Nursing Society (1982) Guidelines for nursing care of patients with altered protective mechanisms: impairment of skin related to radiation therapy *Oncology Nursing Forum*, **9** (3): 115–118

Hilderley, L (1983) Skin care in radiation therapy: A review of the literature *Oncology Nursing Forum*, **10** (1): 51–56

Hassey, K and Rose, C (1982) Altered skin integrity in patients receiving radiation therapy *Oncology Nursing Forum*, **9** (4): 44–50

Margolin, S *et al* (1990) Management of radiation-induced moist skin desquamation using hydrocolloid dressings *Cancer Nursing*, **13** (2): 71–80

Situation Requiring Nursing Intervention

Stomatitis and Mucositis

Common Potential Problems

Pain and discomfort, difficult eating and drinking leading to impaired nutritional and hydrational status, an increased susceptibility to infection and impaired verbal communication.

Nursing Intention

1 Education of the patient in the means of promoting comfort and minimising problems.
2 Maintenance of adequate nutrition.
3 Prevention of oral infection.

Core Care

1 Inform the patient of the probable reasons for stomatitis, and/or mucositis, expected duration of the problem, potential associated problems and self-care measures available to limit these effects.

2 Ensure the patient is aware of the correct techniques when performing oral hygiene and examining the oral cavity. Check for signs of infection and a deterioration in the integrity of the oral mucosa, lips, tongue and dentition daily.

3 Mouthwashes of saline, 1 teaspoonful of salt in 500 ml of water, hydrogen peroxide 1/4 strength (one part hydrogen peroxide to three parts saline, to loosen hardened debris and crusts) and sodium bicarbonate, 1 teaspoonful in 500 ml of water (to remove tenacious mucous) may be used, following liaison with hospital pharmacist concerning the correct dilution. The frequency of mouth washes will be determined by the severity of the stomatitis, but may need to be as often as every 2 hours.

4 Ensure the patient uses a soft toothbrush for cleaning the oral cavity or soft pink toothettes if unable to tolerate a toothbrush; toothpaste will aggravate the discomfort.

5 Advise the patient to minimise potential trauma to the mucous membrane by avoiding coarse, hot and spicy foods. Pain and discomfort may be alleviated with topical and systemic analgesics, lips should be cleansed with saline moistened gauze, and KY Jelly applied to soothe any cracks.

6 Discuss nutritional and hydrational requirements with the patient, suggesting an oral intake of 2 l in 24 hours, soft foods with sauces and gravies and taking plenty of fluids with meals. Initiate a dietetic referral if necessary and monitor the patient's intake, output and a twice weekly weight.

7 Observe the oral cavity for signs of candida and herpes simplex infection, report the presence of these to the medical staff immediately. Prophylactic nystatin rinses may be employed when prescribed.

8 Minimise any impaired communication the patient may be experiencing as a result of the stomatitis and/or mucositis by maintaining frequent oral

hygiene and considering the use of analgesics. Provide the patient with alternative methods of communication such as a writing pad and pencil and a sign board if unable to talk.

Further Reading

Beck, S (1979) Impact of a systematic oral care protocol on stomatitis after chemotherapy *Cancer Nursing*, **2** (3): 185–199

Daeffler, R (1980, 1981) Oral hygiene measures for patients with cancer Part I, II and III *Cancer Nursing* (1980) **3** (5): 347–356 (1980) **3** (6): 427–432 (1981) **4** (1): 24–35

Lindquist, S F *et al* (1978) Effect of oral hygiene on stomatitis in patients receiving chemotherapy *Journal of Prosthetic Dentistry*, **40** (3): 312–314

Oncology Nursing Forum (1982) Guidelines for nursing care of patients with altered protective mechanisms: Stomatitis *Oncology Nursing Forum*, **9** (1): 69–73

Hyland, S (1986) Selecting a tool for measuring stomatitis *Oncology Nursing Forum*, **13** (2): 119–120

Crosby, C (1989) Method in mouth care *Nursing Times*, **85** (35): 38–41

Dudak, L (1987) Mouth care for mucositis due to radiation therapy *Cancer Nursing*, **10** (3): 131–140

CORE CARE PLAN   62

Situation Requiring Nursing Intervention

Altered Taste

Common Potential Problems
Alteration in taste acuity (a decrease or absence), an unpleasant taste leading to a reduced nutritional intake, weight loss and a lack of pleasure in the social experience of eating.

Nursing Intention
1 The patient will maintain an optimum nutritional status to facilitate health in the presence of disease and treatment.
2 Education of the patient concerning adaptation of nutritional intake to minimise unpleasant tastes.

Core Care
1 Perform an assessment with the patient to identify the type and degree of taste alteration, possible physiological or treatment related causes of the taste change and the impact upon nutritional daily intake.
2 Inform the patient of the mechanisms for taste change, expected duration of such changes and self-care measures to diminish the effect of altered taste.
3 Nutritional interventions should be tailored to meet individual needs according to food preferences, habits and side-effects of treatment, but may include:
   - tempting current taste ability with spices, sauces, flavourings and seasonings. These will enhance the aroma of food and thus improve taste
   - concentrating on eating pallatable foods, ensuring an adequate intake of protein
   - providing small, frequent and attractive meals which smell good, and have a pleasing texture
   - taking high protein meals at breakfast, as an alteration in taste is heightened towards the end of the day
   - ensuring the mouth is clean and moist prior to and following meals
   - chilling food may make the food more pallatable.
4 An adequate calorie intake and a balanced diet should be ensured and help sought from the dietitian at every opportunity.
5 Encourage the patient to share his experience with others experiencing taste change, and provide emotional and educational support through open communication and a hopeful attitude.
6 Consider a discussion whereby food and eating are viewed as part of treatment and a necessary activity if patient is to be able to take part in meaningful activities.

Core Care Plans Manual

Further Reading

Dewys, W and Walters, K (1975) Abnormalities of taste sensations in cancer patients *Cancer*, **37**: 1888–1896

Dewys, W (1978) Changes in taste sensation and feeding behaviour in cancer patients: A review *Journal of Human Nutrition*, **32**: 447–454

Huldij, A *et al* (1986) Alteration in taste appreciation in cancer patients during treatment *Cancer Nursing*, **9** (1): 38–42

Shaw, C (1989) A taste of things to come *Nursing Times*, **85** (22): 26–28

Shibbs, L (1989) Taste changes in cancer patients *Nursing Times*, **85** (3): 49–50

Strohl, R (1983) Nursing management of the patient with cancer experiencing taste changes *Cancer Nursing*, **6** (5): 353–359

Tait, N and Aisner, J (1989) Nutritional concerns of cancer patients *Seminars in Oncology Nursing*, **5** (2) Supplement 1: 58–62

Woods, M (1989) Tumour takes all *Nursing Times*, **85** (3): 46–47

Situation Requiring Nursing Intervention

Xerostomia

Common Potential Problems

Taste alteration, difficulty chewing and swallowing, an increased susceptibility to infection and oral discomfort.

Nursing Intention

1 Education of the patient in the ways of promoting comfort, a moist mucosa and minimising problems.

2 Prevention of oral infection.

Core Care

1 Inform the patient of the possible reasons for xerostomia, the expected duration of the problems, potential associated problems and self-care measures available to limit the effects.

2 Ensure the patient is aware of the correct technique when performing oral hygiene and examining the oral cavity. Check for signs of infection and a deterioration in the integrity of oral mucosa daily. Mouthwashes of normal saline, one teaspoonful in 500 ml of water before meals, and as required, may moisten the mouth. Prophylactic nystatin rinses may be used to prevent a candida infection.

3 Ensure the patient takes a high fluid intake of 2–3 l in 24 hours, taking drinks frequently during the day.

4 Lubricating the oral mucosa with artificial saliva and the lips with KY Jelly may be helpful prior to meals and during conversation, in addition sucking hard, flat, sugarless candy may help.

5 Make the patient aware of helpful menu choice such as using sauces, gravies and high moisture foods to aid chewing and swallowing. A dietetic referral may be appropriate if a taste change is also present.

Further Reading

Bersani, G and Carl, W (1983) Oral care for cancer patients *American Journal of Nursing*, **83** (4): 533–536

Regnard, C and Fitton, S (1989) Mouth care: A flow diagram *Palliative Medicine*, **3**: 67–69

Richardson, A (1987) A process standard for oral care *Nursing Times*, **83** (32): 38–40

Sullivan, M and Fleming, T (1983) Oral care for the radiotherapy-treated head and neck cancer patient *Dental Hygiene*, **60** (3): 112–114

Situations Requiring Nursing Intervention

Oral Morphine Sulphate

The administration of oral morphine sulphate solution for chronic pain associated with malignant disease.

Common Potential Problems

Unrelieved pain leading to insomnia, withdrawal from valued activities, depression, anxiety and inability to perform self-care activities, side-effects associated with therapy, for example nausea, constipation, drowsiness, confusion and urinary retention and fears of addiction and/or tolerance.

Nursing Intention

1 Achievement of adequate pain relief.

2 Ensuring the patient reports alterations in pain levels.

3 Minimising side-effects and abating concerns about therapy.

Core Care

1   Prior to and during therapy a pain assessment detailing site, onset, duration, quality, severity and aggravating and alleviating factors should be carried out. A selected pain tool to record a baseline and alterations in levels of pain may be descriptive, numeric or visual analogue in nature, and it should be ensured the patient understands and can use the scale following instruction.

2   Negotiate with the patient graduated realistic goals of pain relief, for example, pain free for sleeping, pain free at rest and finally pain free on movement within an achievable time frame.

3   Administer oral morphine sulphate as prescribed at regular intervals (usually four hourly). If pain is unrelieved or reappears before the next dose further additional doses will be required and the medication dosage and/or frequency should be titrated within the prescribed parameters.

4   Document the degree, onset and duration of pain relief following medication to determine optimal dosage.

5   Encourage the patient to verbalise alterations in levels of pain and observe for signs of ineffective pain relief, for example, facial expression, guarded movements, inability to concentrate, restlessness and difficulty sleeping.

6   Instruct the patient concerning the nature of medication, possible side-effects, self-care for such side-effects, necessity to report changes in pain and the need for regular administration. Provide a written explanation in addition to a verbal presentation.

7   Drowsiness and confusion (muddled thoughts, disorientation and hallucinations) are early effects and should diminish over 7 days. Warn the patient about initial drowsiness and encourage to persevere in the knowledge that it will lessen. Orientate to time, place and person and maintain a safe environment. Drowsiness may be a reflection of pain relief when previously

exhausted mentally and physically from uncontrolled pain. Report excessive and prolonged drowsiness and confusion to the medical officer.

8 If nausea and vomiting occur, administer anti-emetics regularly as prescribed and monitor their effectiveness. Consider modification of the preparation or route of medication if nausea and vomiting remain unresolved, in conjunction with the medical officer.

9 To control any constipation the patient my be experiencing, suggest a high fibre diet, increased fluid intake and regular exercise if possible. In conjunction with the medical officer consider prescription of a regular aperient. Monitor bowel action.

10 Respiratory depression is rarely seen in patients receiving morphine sulphate who have severe pain due to malignant disease, but patients who have a limited respiratory reserve, raised intracranial pressure or chronic obstructive airways disease, should be observed carefully, particularly when the level of pain is dramatically reduced as a result of other pain relieving methods.

11 Explore any fears concerning psychological dependence (addiction) and the development of tolerance. Tolerance is characterised by decreasing efficacy with repeated administration, and it may require an increase in dose to maintain the analgesic effect, but it has been illustrated that with longer durations of opioid adminstration, the slower the rate of increasing the dose. Psychological dependence rarely, if ever, occurs in cancer patients receiving opioids for chronic pain.

12 To complement the pharmacological approach to pain relief, explore previous pain coping methods and non-pharmacological approaches, for example, positioning, heat and cold applications, pressure and massage, relaxation, hypnosis and distraction.

13 Consider physical, psychological, environmental and spiritual dimensions of chronic pain which may need to be addressed with the patient prior to achieving adequate pain relief.

14 When the patient's pain is resistant or semi-responsive to oral morphine sulphate, consider seeking advice from pain specialists (nursing, medical and physiotherapy) and, after consultation with the medical officer, the use of co-analgesics, for example, nonsteroidal anti-inflammatory drugs (for bone pain) and corticosteroids (for nerve compression) may be beneficial.

Further Reading

Anderson, J (1982) Nursing management of the cancer patient in pain: A review of the literature *Cancer Nursing*, **5** (1): 33–41

Archer Copp, L (1985) *Perspectives on Pain: Recent Advances in Nursing* Edinburgh: Churchill Livingstone

Baines, M (1989) Pain relief in active patients with cancer: Analgesic drugs are the foundation of management *British Medical Journal*, **298**: 36–38

Davidson, P (1989) Facilitating coping with cancer pain *Palliative Medicine*, **2** (2): 107–114

Dicks, B (1990) Cancer pain: Assessment of pain *Cancer Nursing*, **13** (14): 256–261

Hanks, G (1987) Opioid analgesics in the management of pain in patients with cancer: A review *Palliative Medicine*, **1** (1): 1–25

Lindley, C and Fields, S (1990) Narcotic analgesics: Clinical pharmacology and therapeutics *Cancer Nursing*, **13** (1): 23–28

McCafferey, M (1985) *Nursing Management of the Patient with Pain* London: Harper and Row

McCafferey, M and Beebe, A (1990) *Pain: A Manual for Nursing Practice* St Louis: C. V. Mosby

McCafferey, M and O'Neil-Page, E (1990) Nurses' knowledge of opioid analgesic drugs and psychological dependence *Cancer Nursing*, **13** (1): 21–27

McGuire, D and Yarbro, C (1987) *Cancer Pain Management* Orlando: Grune and Stratton

McGuire, D (1989) Cancer pain: Pathophysiology of pain in cancer *Cancer Nursing*, **12** (5): 310–315

Raiman, J (1986) Pain relief – a two-way process *Nursing Times*, **82** (15): 24–28

Seers, K (1988) Factors affecting pain assessment *The Professional Nurse*, **3** (6): 201–206

Twycross, R and Lack, S (1983) *Symptoms Control in Far Advanced Cancer: Pain Relief* Edinburgh: Churchill Livingstone

Twycross, R and Lack, S (1987) *Oral Morphine: Information for Patients' Families and Friends* Beaconsfield: Beaconsfield Publishers

Twycross, R *et al* (1990) *Therapeutics in Terminal Cancer* Edinburgh: Churchill Livingstone

Walker, V, Dicks, B and Webb, W (1987) Pain assessment charts in the management of chronic cancer pain *Palliative Medicine*, **1** (2): 111–116

World Health Organisation (1986) *Cancer Pain Relief* Geneva: World Health Organisation

FURTHER READING

Listed below are several texts which the nurse providing care for the oncology patient may find useful. They include information on the aetiology, treatment options and probable needs of a patient with cancer and extensive suggestions concerning appropriate assessment, intervention and evaluation strategies.

Baird, S (1988) *Decision Making in Oncology Nursing* Toronto: B. C. Decker Inc.

Bevers, M, Durbury, S and Werner, J (1984) *Complete Guide to Cancer Nursing* London: Edward Arnold

Brown, M H *et al* (1986) *Standards of Oncology Nursing Practice* New York: McGraw Hill

Burkhalter, P K and Donley, D L (1978) *Dynamics of Oncology Nursing* New York: McGraw Hill

Burns, N (1982) *Nursing and Cancer* Philadelphia: Saunders

Capra, L *et al* (1984) *The Nursing Care of the Patient with Cancer. 2nd Edn.* London: Macmillan

Devita, V T *et al* (1982) *Cancer: Principles and Practice of Oncology* Philadelphia: J. B. Lippincott

Donaghue, M *et al* (1982) *Nutritional Aspects of Cancer Care* Reston: Reston Publishing Inc.

Donovan, M and Girton, S (1984) *Cancer Care Nursing. 2nd Edn.* Norwalk: Appleton-Century-Crofts

Dortman, C S and Goffnet, D R (1980) *Manual of Clinical Problems in Oncology* Boston: Little Brown

Faulkner, A (1990) *Oncology; Excellence in Nursing, The Research Route* London: Scutari Press

Griffiths, M *et al* (1984) *Oncology Nursing: Pathophysiology, Assessment and Intervention* New York: Macmillan

Holmes, S (1988) *Radiotherapy* London: Austen Cornish

Holmes, S (1990) *Chemotherapy* London: Austen Cornish

Johnson, L B and Gross, J (1985) *Handbook of Oncology Nursing* New York: John Wiley

Lauffer, B and Yasko, J (1984) *Care of the Client Receiving Chemotherapy* Reston: Reston Publishing Inc.

Marino, L B (1981) *Cancer Nursing* St. Louis: C. V. Mosby

McCorkle, R and Hongladorum, G (1986) *Issues and Topics in Cancer Nursing* Norwalk: Appleton-Century-Crofts

McIntire, S and Cioppa, A (1984) *Cancer Nursing: A Developmental Approach* New York: John Wiley

FURTHER READING

McNally, J C *et al* (1985) *Guidelines for Cancer Nursing Practice* Orlando: Grune and Stratton

Pritchard, A and David, J (eds) (1988) *Royal Marsden Hospital Manual of Clinical Nursing Procedures 2nd Edn.* London: Harper and Row

Skeel, R T (1989) *Handbook of Cancer Chemotherapy. 2nd Edn.* Boston: Little Brown

Tschudin, V (1989) *Nursing the Patient with Cancer* New York: Prentice Hall

Tiffany, R and Pritchard, P (1988) *Oncology for Nurses and Health Care Professionals. 2nd Edn.* Volume 1: Pathology, Diagnosis and Treatment London: Harper and Row

Tiffany, R and Webb, P (1988) *Oncology for Nurses and Health Care Professionals. 2nd Edn.* Volume 2: Care and Support London: Harper and Row

Tiffany, R and Borley, D (1989) *Oncology for Nurses and Health Care Professionals. 2nd Edn.* Volume 3: Cancer Nursing London: Harper and Row

Vredevoe, D L, Derdiarian, A and Sana, L (1981) *Concepts of Oncology Nursing* New Jersey: Prentice Hall Inc.

Yasko, J M (1982) *Care of the Client Receiving External Radiation Therapy* Reston: Reston Publishing Inc.

Yasko, J M (1983) *Guidelines for Cancer Care: Symptom Management* Reston: Reston Publishing Inc.

Ziegfield, C (1987) *Core Curriculum for Oncology Nursing* Philadelphia: W. B. Saunders

INDEX